TAUGHT BY GOD

Part Two:
GIVEN BY GOD

Printed and bound by Lightning Source UK, Milton Keynes

Published by Crossbridge Books
Tree Shadow, Berrow Green
Martley WR6 6PL
Tel: 01886 821128

© D.J. Bull 2008

First published 2008

All rights reserved. No part of this publication may be reproduced, stored in a retrieval system, or transmitted in any form or by any means – electronic, mechanical, photocopying, recording or otherwise – without prior permission of the Publisher.

ISBN 978 0 9549708 9 5

British Library cataloguing in Publication Data.
A catalogue record for this book is available
from the British Library.

Also published by Crossbridge Books:

Saved by God Dave Bull
It's True! Trevor Dearing
The God of Miracles Trevor and Anne Dearing
Called to Be a Wife Anne Dearing
The Reluctant Bride Kamala Sabaratnam
First Century Close-ups Roger Penney
Schizophrenia Defeated James Stacey
Stepping-Stone Miracles Des Morton
Costly Roots Sarah Cohen
Mountains on the Moon Michael Arthern
Sacred Instinct Allie Ituen

Taught by God
A Trilogy

Book Two:
GIVEN BY GOD

DAVE BULL

BOOK ONE: SAVED BY GOD
BOOK TWO: GIVEN BY GOD
BOOK THREE: HEARD BY GOD

CROSSBRIDGE BOOKS

Publisher's Note

This book is published posthumously. Sadly, Dave Bull died in the spring of 2008, before this second volume of his trilogy could be published. I met Dave in 2007, and I know that he is greatly missed by all who knew him. But I feel that our loss is Heaven's gain.

Eileen Mohr
Editor and publisher

Scripture quotations used in this book are from the
HOLY BIBLE, NEW INTERNATIONAL VERSION.
Copyright © 1973, `978, 1984 by
International Bible Society.
Used with permission.

Book Two:

GIVEN BY GOD
Receiving inspiration from the Word of God

"... All your sons will be taught by the Lord,
and great will be your children's peace."
(Isaiah 54: 13)

"[Jesus said:] It is written
in the prophets:
'They will be taught by God.' "
(John 6: 45)

Acknowledgements

Once again, I am indebted to Eileen Mohr. From her editing of the first book I learned how surprisingly easy it is for one or two ill-chosen words to imply something different from the intended meaning. This second book gives me the opportunity to give my thanks to some more people.

I want to thank Bob and Marie for their shepherding when I was called back into the Church with my dear friend Andy Spriggs, who is now with the Lord. I am grateful to Menna and Bob Collier, two special Christian friends, who showed great patience as house-group hosts while I was first learning how to teach.

We are fortunate here at Walton-on-the-Naze to enjoy the services of a number of retired ministers. The Revd Tony Noles, who was the leader of a dynamic and fast-growing Baptist Church in East London, has proved a valuable sounding board for some of my writing. His preaching, along with that of the Revd Colin Noyes and the Revd Tony Pugsley, together with the leadership of our vicar, the Revd Tim Fletcher, are a constant source of inspiration to me.

Of course, thanks must go to my mother for bringing me into a church-going family. Her prayers during my illness-fraught childhood no doubt saved my life. I must also voice my gratitude to my brother Jim, who has been a solid rock to Mum since our father was called to be with the Lord.

D.J.B.

Introduction

So, we have new life in Jesus Christ; what do we do now? Well, I believe Christians have two duties. We need to be regularly inspired by what God has to say to us in His Word, and we need to acquire the habit of being still before our heavenly Father in prayer. In this second part of the series, we shall consider how to profitably study the Bible; the final book discusses our times of prayer. The second and third books also give me the opportunity to expand some of the topics that were only covered briefly in Book 1.

The Bible is a spiritual book for spiritual people; it provides the necessary nourishment for our regenerated human spirits. Understanding comes when this spiritual food has been properly digested. We do not have to believe in the Bible; we are to believe in the One whom the Bible reveals to us. The purpose of the Bible is to show us Jesus and inspire us to be closer to Him. It will then guide us in our ongoing relationship with our Lord. The Bible is therefore not a book to help us become better geologists, palaeontologists, historians or humanists. At a very young age, I was presented with the Scriptures and was told that everything within is the Word of God. I have now arrived at the stage where I can accept this with all my heart.

You will find no 'higher' or 'lower' Bible criticism here: as I say, we shall be studying a spiritual book. When you consider our Lord's first disciples, how many of them do you think would get through today's theological training colleges? Having said that, I am sure that the apostle Paul would pass with honours! I completely agree with J C Ryle when he said: "A humble and prayerful spirit will find a thousand things in the Bible which the proud, self-conceited student will utterly fail to discern."

My aim is to stimulate expectancy in those who are prepared to regularly and prayerfully 'search the Scriptures'. While prayer is the way that we talk to God, the Bible is one way in which God speaks to us. Reading the Word of God is the main means by which we build up our faith, and faith is the key that opens up a life in fellowship with our risen Saviour. In Jesus, the words of the Bible became flesh and dwelt among us. In Him, and only in Him, can God's Word again become flesh and dwell in us.

I pray that my joy in God's Word is infectious, and that it may be caught from the pages of this book!

"... Scripture cannot be broken"
(John 10: 35)

"For the Word of God is living and active.
Sharper than any two-edged sword,
it penetrates even to dividing soul and spirit,
joints and marrow;
it judges the thoughts and attitudes
of the heart."
(Heb 4: 12)

Contents

Section		Page
1	Bible Authority	1
2	A Spiritual Book	8
3	The Make Up of Scripture	16
4	Our Approach to the Word	27
5	Example of Bible Study (1)	35
	The Old Testament (History)	
6	Example of Bible Study (2)	43
	The Old Testament (Poetry)	
7	Example of Bible Study (3)	51
	The Old Testament (Prophets)	
8	Grace and Peace	59
9	Example of Bible Study (4)	68
	The Gospels	
10	Example of Bible Study (5)	73
	The New Testament Letters	
11	What Contradictions?	80
12	The Liberal Church	99
Epilogue		110

"Then the Word became flesh
and made His dwelling among us."
(John 1: 14)

"You diligently study the Scriptures
because you think that by them
you possess eternal life.
These are the Scriptures that testify
about Me, yet you refuse
to come to Me to have life."
(John 5: 39-40)

Section One

Bible Authority

How can we believe that the Bible is the Word of God? Can we prove it? Well, of course, the answer to that has to be no. While the Holy Spirit will leave you in no doubt that you are reading God's Word, you will probably not be able to pass on that certainty to others. Because each one of us is different, we are each to have our own special rapport with God. Unlike other faiths, Christianity is not a religion; it is a vital, ongoing relationship with a Person, our Lord Jesus Christ. As such, our authority for the Word of God has to come directly from Him.

We know that Jesus always spoke the truth. He would not accommodate our limited understanding by adjusting the truth. He would correct any misunderstandings that His followers might have had (Mark 10: 35-45). Whenever the disciples would be unable to understand Him with their human limitations, He said so (John 16: 12). Hence, we can believe in evil because Jesus drove out evil from those possessed by it; Jesus would not humour a false belief. By that same token, we can believe in the Scriptures, especially the Old Testament, because Jesus vouched for their authenticity

Jesus quoted with authority from nearly every book of the Old Testament; He affirmed their truth by saying,

SECTION 1

"The Scriptures cannot be broken" (John 10: 35). Many times Jesus said that things happened *"so that Scripture might be fulfilled"* (John 13: 18). When confronted with Satan's tempting, Jesus quoted Scripture as the final word on the subject (Luke 4: 4). Even Satan knew the power of Scripture, and tried to misuse it to his own advantage (Luke 4:10,11).

The authorities in some countries are terrified of the Bible's power; they will not let a single copy cross their borders. May God protect our brothers and sisters who have to read their Bibles with the threat of persecution hanging over them!

We hear stories of how those in power in some communist countries have rewritten their histories in order to paint themselves in a better light. If the Israelites had fabricated the Old Testament, would they not have made it far more flattering? Wouldn't the proud Jews have appeared far more noble and obedient to their special God? As it stands, many Jewish scholars find some passages very difficult to explain. This is especially true in the case of the Suffering Servant (Isaiah 53), which is a graphic picture of Jesus. The fact that the Old Testament was written in anticipation of Jesus is unquestioningly confirmed. Jesus wanted people to search the Old Testament Scriptures in order that they might find Him revealed in their pages (John 5: 38-39).

But what about the New Testament – *"Then the Word became flesh and made His dwelling among us"*? (John 1: 14). In Jesus, the promises contained within the Old Testament pages were brought to life. We have four full, detailed, eyewitness accounts of the good news of how our Father reconciled sinful man to Himself through the life and death of Jesus. The word 'Gospel' means 'good news'.

The Gospels are the 'good seed' about which Jesus expounded in the Parable of the Sower. The Holy Spirit sows this seed with the help of the apostles, evangelists, ministers and ordinary believers in the hope of finding fertile soil in the

Bible Authority

hearts of those hearing the Word (Matt 13: 18-23). It is from hearing the Word that the gift of faith is received (Rom 10: 17), and without faith it is impossible to believe in or please God (Heb 11: 6).

To approach the Gospels in a critical frame of mind would not be helpful if we wish to learn from them. To my knowledge, the negative criticism that has been written about them has been shown, on further examination, to have been misguided. The Gospels' authority validates itself. If we try to test or disprove them, instead it is they that test us. As for Jesus' words, almost no one has ever criticised any of them! Jesus is the life and light of the Scriptures. As Robert Murray McCheyne has said, "When you are reading a book in a dark room and find it difficult, you take it to a window to get more light. So take your Bible to Christ."

Jesus knew that His words would never die (Matt 24: 35). He knew that the Gospel would reach every nation. When He was commending the woman for anointing Him with very expensive perfume, He said: *"I tell you the truth, wherever this Gospel is preached throughout the world, what she has done will also be told, in memory of her"* (Matt 26: 13). *"And the Gospel must be preached to all nations"* (Mark 13: 10).

One line from a Gospel – on a Christmas card, for example – can be a seed prayerfully planted that may germinate some time later. This can have far more effect than a sermon from us to an unwilling hearer.

Jesus tells us that whenever the Gospel is preached, Satan will try to snatch the seed before it has a chance to take root. Satan will suggest that this message should be ridiculed and ignored. In the parable, this is the seed that is sown onto the path (Matt 13: 19).

Some may welcome the Gospel following an emotional letdown. A loved-one may have departed, or a general feeling of insecurity may have allowed the seed into their heart.

SECTION 1

However, because of the lack of good Christian teaching and fellowship, the good news is not deep-rooted in the Person of Jesus. Such a new believer's faith proves to be only temporary, and when persecution or opposition come, the seed dries up. This is like the seed that falls onto the rocks (Matt 13: 20-21).

Others allow worldly issues to grow alongside the kingdom seed. Worries and greed choke the Word that grows among such "thorns" (Matt 13: 22).

Let's thank God that His seed has found a home in the fertile soil of your heart! Now, it can be multiplied; it can reproduce itself. It is so sad that most Christians do not progress beyond being babies in Christ. My prayer is that you will take in the solid food of God's Word and grow into maturity. You can then become a disciple. Through God's Word, your life will have direction and power. God will be able to use you as His beloved, faithful child; you will then bear much fruit for His kingdom.

Jesus wants us to raise a plentiful harvest for His kingdom. For this to happen, we must allow the Gospel of God to be broadcast. This work of broadcasting must always be done prayerfully and be accompanied by caring pastoral work under the supervision of the Holy Spirit.

In the rest of the New Testament, we find two of the writers that God entrusted with the Gospels have further entries. Luke, the doctor who was empowered to write the third Gospel, was also given authority to account for the rapid and massive growth of the early Church by writing the Acts of the Apostles. Similarly, John, the writer of the fourth Gospel, was entrusted with the Revelation of Jesus Christ. He is also responsible for the letters that bear his name.

The teaching letters of Paul take up much of the remainder of the New Testament. The apostle Peter vouched for the authority of Paul's letters. In his own scriptural letter, he writes, *"His* [Paul's] *letters contain some things that are hard to*

Bible Authority

understand, which ignorant and unstable people distort, as they do other Scriptures, to their own destruction" (2 Peter 3: 16). Peter's use of that word "other" shows that he includes Paul's letters with the rest of the Scriptures, and thereby gives them their special authority.

Apart from the apostle Peter's own letters, we are left with Hebrews (which traditionally was attributed to Paul; this is now disputed) and the letters of James and Jude.

But it is the testimony of thousands of Christian believers over the last two thousand years, people who have taken God at His word and trusted in and preached the Scriptures – these people have known them to be the inspired Word of God. They would not seek, nor would they need, any proof of the Bible's authority. To preachers such as Wesley, Spurgeon, Moody ... the list is endless; the Bible is unquestionably the living Word of God, the spiritual Word of God and the voice and power of their Saviour, Jesus Christ, because they continually experienced its power in their own lives and in the lives of those who responded to their preaching. May it be so for you!

So, can you know with any certainty that the Bible is the Word of God and not merely an anthology of the thoughts of Middle-Eastern men? As I have said, our Lord must be your ultimate authority, but there are a number of things you should consider: We have briefly discussed the honesty of the Scriptures, how the proud, exclusive Israelites would not have invented these self-incriminating accounts. The writings also displayed a single-eyed fearlessness that confronted sinful rulers – openly condemning powerful despots – something that few men would dare to do. Human minds could not have possibly foreseen and written the numerous prophecies that were later fulfilled, spanning the centuries, while displaying such an amazing unity of purpose. The Bible describes a purity that is completely alien to man. Indeed the unveiling of this purity can turn the world of stubborn mankind upside down.

SECTION 1

What mortal could write doctrines that an obedient fisherman can be taught to grasp, but which the complex minds of philosophers and scientists completely fail to see? What man could have written with such heart-searching power that can completely ransack your conscience? Yes, only the Bible can search your heart, revealing spiritual laws about which unredeemed souls can know nothing. Who on earth could have thought up laws that none but the offending conscience can convict? And yet, who but God could also compose words that can both comfort your heart and raise your dejected spirit? And what mortal could have written words that can convert your contrite heart while convincing you to follow the only possible source of those words, your loving, heavenly Father, as revealed in His risen Son?

May the Lord Jesus commend His Word to your heart through His life-giving Spirit! May you daily so hunger and thirst for the Word, may you hold it as so precious, that your Father may be glorified through your obedience to it!

Prayer: *Heavenly Father, thank You for giving us Your Word. May it be for me a daily assurance of Your presence with me! May it be a constant reminder of Your love for me! And may it be my daily nourishment of solid spiritual food to preserve me in Your kingdom during my journey here on earth. I ask this in Jesus' holy name. Amen.*

"...But when He, the Spirit of truth comes, He will guide you into all truth ..."

(John 16: 12)

"I have hidden Your Word in my heart that I might not sin against You."

(Psalm 119: 11)

Section Two

A Spiritual Book

The Bible is a spiritual book. However, we are not born spiritual people – not any more. This is not the way that God had originally planned it, for we are made body, soul and spirit (1 Thess 5: 23). One of the first things that God says to us in His Word is the fact that mankind is fallen, separated from God. One consequence of this is that man's spirit, the place where God would have us commune with Him (John 4: 24), has become almost ineffectual or dormant due to the inflation of his soul or ego.

In order for us to be in a position to fully take in God's spiritual Word, a transformation has to take place deep within us. We need to be born again (John 3: 3). Our spirits need to be enlivened so that we can receive spiritual things from God. Until this transformation happens, God's Word may seem to be a grey, lifeless, inaccessible book. While I can remember always being in awe of the Bible, I used to believe that the data was handed down verbally from generation to generation and that it probably contained some errors.

When I gave my life to Jesus and my spirit was reborn, passages that I had previously thought of as being dubious suddenly became meaningful. Great chunks of God's Word that

A Spiritual Book

I had previously put down as error now made powerful sense.
When we are reborn, God's Holy Spirit takes up residence in our revived human spirits (Romans 8: 9). One of the first tasks of the Holy Spirit is to correct our consciences so that they are in line with God's Word. This is done while giving due consideration to our level of maturity (1 Cor 8: 9-12). From this moment on, we have the true author of Scripture always at our disposal. This is how previously vague passages become clear. As we become more spiritual, God's Word becomes more accessible. This is the result of the continual enlightenment of the indwelling Holy Spirit. Our spirits can then feed our soulish minds, and this promotes understanding.

Some evangelicals will dispute the above. Some will contend that the Bible is sufficiently clear for all to read and understand the message it contains. Well, that is not what the Bible says about itself. 1 Corinthians Chapter 2 addresses this point, summing it all up in verses 13 and 14: *"This is what we speak, not in words taught us by human wisdom but in words taught by the Spirit, expressing spiritual truths in spiritual words. The man without the Spirit does not accept the things that come from the Spirit of God, for they are foolishness to him, and he cannot understand them, because they are spiritually discerned."*

Some will no doubt then ask about Old Testament times, when people did not have the indwelling Holy Spirit. How did they understand God's Word? Well, except when one of God's anointed or His Spirit-filled prophets expounded the Word, they did not understand it. Take Josiah, for instance. The Word of God was rediscovered while the temple was being repaired. When the Word was read out to Josiah, he had to enquire of the prophet just what it all meant. His intellect could tell that something was wrong, but the Spirit-filled prophet had to bring the Word to life for him. Unlike the Gnostics, I am not talking about mysteries being revealed that are not in the Bible. No, I

SECTION 2

am simply talking about the Bible being made accessible to us. As Job says, *"It is the Spirit in a man, the breath of the Almighty, that gives him understanding"* (Job 32: 8). Martin Luther tells us, "Proper understanding of the Scriptures comes only through the Holy Spirit. If God does not open and explain the Holy Writ, no one can understand it; it will remain a closed book, enveloped in darkness."

> Long my imprisoned spirit lay
> Fast bound in sin and nature's night;
> Thine eye diffused a quickening ray,
> I woke, the dungeon flamed with light;
> My chains fell off, my heart was free;
> I rose, went forth, and followed Thee.
> (Charles Wesley)

Yes, our spirits were indeed imprisoned. The faculties of our spirits, our consciences, our ability to receive through Divine intuition and our means of spiritual communion were fast bound by our sinful natures, while all the time our fallen egos held dominance. God had therefore no access into our lives. Thanks to Jesus, and our spiritual rebirth, we are now temples of God. Now the dungeon flames with light; our spirits have become the Holy of Holies of our own rebuilt temple. Each day we are being made ever more holy. The Holy of Holies was the most sacred place of the old earthly temple. Now that we are God's temples, our enlivened spirits have become our Holy of Holies, indwelt by the Holy Spirit of God.

Henceforth, our Bible becomes our special, priceless treasure – an inexhaustible supply of love, comfort, wisdom, help, strength, revitalisation and much, much more besides. We can now tap into true wisdom. However, the Holy Spirit must keep our pride in check, for pride is now correctly seen to be the greatest sin. Satan can make us think that we have

A Spiritual Book

'sussed' the Bible by our own cleverness. He can have a field day fuelling our pride! He can make us feel that we are greatly superior beings, unlike 'those ignorant, faithless sinners'. The Holy Spirit must keep us in mind of the fact that we are sinners and that we receive all we have freely from God, in the saving power of Jesus Christ. We can have no cause for boasting (Eph 2: 8-9).

Let's face it: the idea of God dying for our sins on the cross is nonsense! The Bible seems, at first, to agree (1 Cor 1: 21), but look at verse 25: *"For the foolishness of God is wiser than man's wisdom, and the weakness of God is stronger than man's strength"*. Without spiritual help, the Christian message is indeed foolishness. Religious people look for a miraculous sign from God to help them believe; to them, the cross is a display of failure and weakness; it becomes an obstacle in the path of their faith. Clever, intelligent people look for wisdom; to them, the cross is foolishness. So if there is a spark inside you, enabling you to believe in the message of the cross, then you must have been spiritually given that spark; otherwise, you too would probably reject the cross as nonsense!

Having said that, many early civilisations have legends of a virgin giving birth and sacrificial appeasement for sins. Those civilisations had welcomed Satan into their ceremonies. He had indoctrinated their 'truths'. As a result, we have practices such as human sacrifices, cannibalism, the drinking of blood, child sacrifices, female circumcision and all sorts of other atrocities supposedly instigated by God to appease His displeasure. As I have said elsewhere, Satan seldom talks absolute rubbish when referring to God; he will tweak the truth just enough to send people off on the wrong track. He will then be sure to keep them away from the right track. There is only one appeasement for our sins, and this is clearly set out in the spiritual, uncontaminated Word of God.

SECTION 2

I have said that the spirit of an unregenerated person has been completely dominated by his or her soul. This is true. That person is effectively dead to God. However, in a very small minority of cases, the soul has not dominated the spirit. This is true of those involved in the occult, witchcraft or spiritualism. These people are indeed dead to God, but very much alive to Satan! Yes, everybody has a conscience, but for non-Christians, it is not the voice of God. How could it be? If it were the voice of God, all consciences would agree. While most consciences in western civilisation will agree on the basics – do no murder, do not steal, and do not lie – for other things, most people instinctively adjust their own conscience with the best they know, or very often what is most accommodating, and this 'best' is forever changing.

A person might feel a twinge of conscience after walking past a beggar. After maybe discussing this with friends, someone might suggest that beggars only spend their money on drink. So, the next time a beggar is confronted, the conscience will remain calm – until that is, a new 'best' is suggested and that takes its turn in the non-believer's conscience. Christians have their regenerated spirits safeguarded by the indwelling Holy Spirit, who ensures that our consciences are always kept in line with God's Word. As we consent to this, God's Word can also penetrate our hearts and influence our desires.

I said in the first book that only God could address the spirit of a man. This is also true, but He can and does use His spiritual teachers and preachers if they are open to Him. When I first started to teach, I did so after much preparation. I was leading by my notes. However, all that the people were getting was 'me'. If I had read something interesting that week, my teaching might be interesting. If I felt a bit tired, the whole evening would be a bit tired. Sometimes people would be kind enough to say that I had really helped them. I was of course delighted – after all, they were praising me! In fact, when I found out just what had actually helped them, I could never remember saying those things! After feeling the urge to expand a given point, I must have looked up from my notes and in so doing allowed God to have an input. I eventually arrived at the stage where I trusted God for every moment of my teaching.

I am not saying that teaching or preaching has to be spontaneous in order to be spiritual: it simply has to be from God. A preacher who uses his mind to assemble his sermon, calling on concordances, commentaries and the like, is only likely to affect a listening mind – mind addresses mind; spirit addresses spirit – whereas a preacher who would not dare to begin his notes until he has spent time before God on any given subject will probably find that inspiration will flow from him.

In the early days of our spirituality, we may find that Christian writers seem to play a large part in opening up the Scriptures for us. We may find this surprising. We may wonder why the Word of God seems to need the help of such people. I can remember benefiting greatly from twentieth-century writers such as Oswald Chambers, Andrew Murray, Watchman Nee and Colin Urquhart, and then from earlier inspirational works by C H Spurgeon, William Gurnall, Matthew Henry and John Wesley, to name but a few.

I believe that the role of such writers stems from our need of fellowship. We need to realise our dependency on other Christians. I think we are entitled to question the credentials of anyone seeking to be a Christian in isolation. God has so arranged the distribution of His spiritual gifts – gifts such as healing, prophecy, knowledge and wisdom – that we are incomplete without fellowship with those having these gifts (1 Cor 12). This is why only group or corporate prayers will answer some of our needs. This is why some of our healing will only be achieved through one who has been given this spiritual gift. This is why some of our mind-related problems may only be uncovered by a member of the Church who has the

SECTION 2

spiritual gift of knowledge. Each congregation should expect spiritual gifts to be in operation. Happily, these gifts are manifest in many of our churches, even if they may not be recognised as spiritual gifts. I think this is the true meaning of Christian unity: namely, our need of each other in fellowship. Unlike many, I believe Christian unity has nothing to do with the coming together of different denominations, most of which may well have good reasons to remain separate.

The writers that helped open up the Scriptures for me had the spiritual gift of teaching. Every Church fellowship needs at least one with this gift. The difference between one who has a secular talent for teaching and one with this spiritual gift will be immediately apparent. The spiritually gifted will show Jesus in a greater light and make the Bible more accessible; those with a natural talent for teaching will merely appear to be clever or knowledgeable, and instil in us a desire to accumulate knowledge.

Just as the Holy Spirit will show us more of Jesus, each spiritually gifted person should do the same. Christian writers should draw people to the Scriptures, but they must never claim equality with them; nor should we see their writings as acceptable alternatives to the Scriptures.

Prayer: *Heavenly Father, I pray that You will encourage each of Your Churches to eagerly seek all the gifts that You have for them. I especially pray for those gifted by You to teach Your Word, that they may glorify You and show more of Jesus Your Son, who is our living Word, and in whose name I ask. Amen.*

"In the past God spoke to our forefathers
through the prophets
at many times and in various ways,
but in these last days
He has spoken to us by His Son ..."
(Heb 1: 1-2)

"...These things happened to them
as examples and were written down as
warnings for us,
on whom the fulfilment
of the ages has come."
(1 Cor 10: 11)

Section Three

The Make up of the Bible

As you know, the Bible is not just one book, or even two books bound together: it is a holy library. And, yes: there is sense and order in the way the various books have been assembled! I shall begin by looking at the Old Testament. Most students of the Bible divide the Old Testament into three sections: the 'History' books, the 'Poetical' books and the Prophets; this is the order in which they appear.

The first fifteen (many say sixteen) books of the Bible narrate the history of God's people from Creation (Genesis 1) to the return of the Israelites from captivity in Babylon and the rebuilding of the temple (Nehemiah). From this rebuilding of the temple, there was to be a four hundred year period of biblical silence before all the fulfilment of the New Testament begins.

The chart on pages 21-22 chronologically tabulates the most important Old Testament events; it shows in which book of the Bible each of these is to be found. We can also see in the table how there are pictures or images of Jesus in each situation. The examples given only scratch the surface, as representations of Jesus are on almost every page of Scripture.

When we study the 'history' section of the Bible, we tend to focus more on the things that happened, rather than on what has been said. Many of the spiritual truths learnt in the New Testament can be seen acted out in the Old Testament history pages. The Old Testament shows us the consequences of the Fall, and the hopelessness of unsaved man's attempts to live up to the high standards of God's righteousness. It is a picture of failure. The Law was put in place to make people aware of their need of a saviour. All of the old Scriptures point towards Jesus. All of the appointed sacrifices are images of Jesus. However, we see false prophets who would tell the people the things they wanted to hear instead of the truth as revealed by the prophets of God. We see religious leaders unable to perceive the love and compassion that were contained within the Law. Only Jesus could fulfil the Law. We cannot work to earn God's favour; we can never deserve His love. Both of these things are now freely ours because we have shown trust in God's eternal remedy for sin, Jesus Christ.

We hear some Christians disputing over whether it is okay for God's saved people to continue to do this thing, and whether they are allowed to do that thing. They are looking in the wrong direction! If people want to be bound by laws, they would be better off attending a synagogue! They might as well remain within the Old Testament pages, for they are certainly not looking at Jesus. We can do nothing to enter the Kingdom of God; Jesus is concerned about what we become. If, like the rich man, we ask Jesus what we must do, then Jesus can only answer in a legal way and recite the commandments (Matt 19: 16-22). Instead, we are to become His followers, His disciples. Jesus died to free us from the Law, and yet people still talk as if they are bound by it. There is now only one condemnation, and that is reserved for those who refuse to step into the light that is Jesus Christ. People who prefer darkness because their deeds are evil shut themselves out of the dimension of Jesus.

We must each allow Jesus to speak to our hearts by reading His Word and listening to His Holy Spirit. As I have said, your conscience is brought more in line with God's Word as you mature. Nobody else can be your conscience, and you cannot be anybody else's conscience. God develops each one of us at our own speed in proportion to the permission that we give Him. No one who regularly comes into the presence of God will continue to do things that are against His Word, but this is not a case of permission or lack of it; it is rather a case of 'seeing' with the eye of our spirit, our conscience. Once these things are seen, they will be repulsive to us.

SECTION 3

I am certain that no words will need to be spoken at the final 'Day of Judgement'. People that are finally exposed to the Light – people confronted with the presence of Jesus for the first time, will know instantly how tainted they are without any need of words.

Moving on with our discussion of the Old Testament: the six (or five) poetical books that follow are collections of spiritual insights: Esther shows how God arranges the circumstances of our lives. We must be watchful and trust in His providence. Most people consider Esther to be the final 'history' book, but I have difficulty in accepting this book as Israel's history. Job addresses the question of why there is evil and suffering in the world. The Psalms are a collection of spiritual prayers and worship; many consider this the most precious of all the old writings. Proverbs is a digest of spiritual wisdom. This book shows that spiritual advice is timeless, and remains accurate throughout history. Ecclesiastes shares the thoughts of a worldly person as he begins to become spiritual. This book re-evaluates 'everything under the sun'. Finally, in this section, the Song of Songs is a picture of the love of Christ for His Church.

Perhaps an extra word should be said about Ecclesiastes. Many wonder why this book is included in the Scriptures, as it appears to be very unspiritual. I believe that we all have to go through our own Ecclesiastes experience on our journey to the cross of Jesus. We each have to realise that *"everything under the sun is meaningless and chasing after the wind"*. It is a short step from this to giving our lives to Jesus at His cross. I believe that this book is a picture of human wisdom almost at the point of becoming spiritual and enlightened. Many on the verge of becoming complete Christians enjoy Ecclesiastes. To me, it has the same appeal as Romans Chapter 7, where Paul explains his human despair before realising just what he has been given in Jesus Christ.

We now turn to the prophets. These we can divide into two sections. We first have the Major Prophets: Isaiah, Jeremiah (who wrote Lamentations), Ezekiel and Daniel; then we have the Minor Prophets: Hosea to Malachi. It must be remembered that prophecies are not always given as a continuous story from beginning to end.

The Make up of the Bible

The visions may not be complete in themselves or in chronological sequence. The most popular secular 'prophet' is Nostradamus. I don't wish to give an opinion of his work, but I note that the main problem his interpreters have is trying to arrange his writings into any kind of order; it is generally agreed that they were not chronological.

Two of the best-known prophets, Elijah and Elisha, do not have eponymous books of Scripture. This is also true of Moses and John the Baptist, arguably the greatest prophets. However, it was Moses' inspired hand that wrote the first five books of the Bible, the Pentateuch. We should remember that to 'prophesy' means to speak forth from God; it does not necessarily mean to foretell the future.

The table on pages 21-22 also shows in block capitals the events in the history of Israel that had an influence on God's subsequent dealings with His people; these events were usually followed by a new covenant. I have deliberately left out any references to end times, as this can only serve to confuse at this stage. These events were the 'crunch times' in the history of the Israelites, during and following which, people showed greater awareness of their need of God's help, forgiveness and deliverance. They are also times where images of Jesus abound.

A single prophetic vision can be descriptive of more than one of these events. God's Word remains constant in all ages and in all situations. Therefore, if you consider a prophecy that contemporaries of the prophet correctly attribute to, say, the forthcoming exile of Israel into Babylon; the words of that same prophecy can be equally intended for people of this age as a reference to the final judgement of God.

This is also true of God's blessings. Visions given foreseeing Jesus' first incarnation can also be descriptive of His future second coming. I believe there is an example of this in

SECTION 3

the prophecy of Malachi, where he tells us that Elijah would precede the coming of the Messiah (Mal 4: 5). Jesus confirmed that John the Baptist was the fulfilment of that prophecy, yet Jesus also said, *"Elijah comes and will restore all things"* (Matt 17: 11). This probably means that Elijah will also be involved in our Lord's awaited return, and that the passage in Malachi was descriptive of both events.

Following on from these prophetic writings there was a period of biblical silence lasting about 400 years after the Israelites rebuilt the temple. Arriving at the New Testament, we come first to the Gospels. The first Gospel in the Bible was written initially for the Jews. It is appropriate that Matthew forms this bridge between the two Testaments; he often used such phrases as, *"... this fulfils what was written* [in the Old Testament]". This Gospel concentrates on the Kingship of Jesus, who is here portrayed as a lion. Jesus is seen as the 'Lion of Judah'. Matthew goes to great lengths to prove Jesus' kingly credentials by stating His royal lineage all the way from David (giving his genealogy from Abraham), in accordance with Old Testament prophecy.

Mark's Gospel emphasises Jesus the Man, as well as Jesus the miracle-worker and servant of God. Luke, a doctor, features Jesus' compassion as healer, shepherd and the one true sacrifice of God. John's Gospel, however, flies above this worldly kingdom and is the most spiritual of the four, symbolised as it is by a soaring eagle. The first three Gospels are called the 'synoptic' Gospels, which means that they were written and are seen from the same viewpoint. John is more analytical, more reflective ... deeper and above all, more spiritual.

We can see the Gospel Word of Jesus represented in the prophecies of Ezekiel and in Revelation. In Ezekiel, we are given a picture of four "living creatures" around the throne of

The Make up of the Bible

THE "HISTORY" BOOKS

Book	Sample Event	Picture of Jesus
Genesis	Creation	Active in creation
	Eden	Fruit – Tree of life

THE FALL

	Enoch	Walked with God

THE FLOOD

	Noah	Salvation
	Abraham	Intercessor/Father
	Isaac	Sacrificial Son
	Jacob	Bridegroom
	Joseph	Alive from dead

SLAVERY

Exodus	Moses	Leading from slavery

SECTION 3

THE LAW

Leviticus	Code	Obedience to God
Numbers	Manna from heaven	Bread of Life
Deuteronomy	Sanctuary	Budded staff
Joshua	Promised Land	Leader
Judges	Samson/Delilah	Nazirite
Ruth	David's family	Redeemer
1 Samuel	Samuel	Obedient child
2 Samuel	David	King/Shepherd
1 Kings/Chron.	Solomon	Wisdom of God
2 Kings/Chron.	Elijah	Ascension
	Elisha	Spirit-filled

EXILE

Ezra	Return from captivity	Prophecy fulfilled
Nehemiah	Rebuild	New Jerusalem

[400 years silence]

MESSIAH

New Testament	Life of Jesus	God with us

THE FALL OF JERUSALEM

Church Age	The 'Night'	Body of Christ

The Make up of the Bible

God, obedient to the Spirit. Each creature had four faces: the face of a man, an ox, a lion and an eagle (Ezek 1: 10). In Revelation we are given another picture. There are again four creatures, but this time one has the head of a man, one has the head of an ox, one has the head of a lion and one has the head of an eagle (Rev 4: 6-8). These visions show that Christ is completely represented by the four Gospels, and that these Gospels carry with them all the spiritual power that is before the throne of God.

It is fitting that the account of the growth of the Church (The Acts of the Apostles) should follow the Gospels. This book could also be entitled 'The Acts of the Holy Spirit', as it shows the tremendous growth and vitality of the new Spirit-filled Church.

It is also fitting that the most complete theological discourse in the Bible is the first of the teaching letters. Romans contains the fullest account of our salvation in Jesus because Paul had not met the recipients of this letter. His other letters were sent to Churches that he had personally planted or that he had helped grow into maturity. Following Paul's other letters and Hebrews, we have letters from James, Peter, John and Jude.

Revelation follows these letters. This last book of the Bible, the last word, is a difficult book and one that should be read in the same way that we read the prophets. I don't claim to understand all of Revelation, but I do believe that it is an important part of the complete Word of God. We should all be aware of the warning given to those who would add to, or take away from, the Holy Scriptures given to us by God (Rev 22: 18,19).

Of course, there is more to Bible study than simply knowing what is in the Scriptures: the Word must enter our heart – we need to be spiritually fed. Rather amusingly, John Blanchard has said: "There is more to Christian growth than

SECTION 3

knowing what the Bible says; nobody is ever nourished by memorising menus." To this, D L Moody can add: "The Scriptures were not given to increase our knowledge but to change our lives."

Prayer: *Heavenly Father, please help me to become fully acquainted with Your Word and its layout. May it become really familiar to me as I get into the habit of trusting it as Your given Word! I ask this in Jesus' name. Amen.*

Perhaps a word could be added here about *The Bible Code*. When the first book was released, a few people asked for my comments. I had to say that I was far from excited. For a long time I have been convinced that the Bible is the Word of God. The fact that it may or may not contain prophetic messages hidden within its pages, messages that only a high-speed computer could unravel, was hardly going to change my life. As I said at the time, if somebody were to give me a twenty-pound note, I would be grateful and begin to think about what I would spend the money on. If that person then walked me to a window in order to show me that the note carries a watermark, I would not be any more grateful. I had no doubt in the first place that the note was real. If the Bible does have a 'watermark' – fine, but it is not something that I expect to be able to use.

Actually, the Bible does have a 'watermark'! I am grateful to my fellow-parishioner and organist, Claude Stokes, for filling in the gaps in my knowledge of this. In an article for our parish magazine, Claude informs us that, in 1982, Dr Eli Rep of the University of Jerusalem and Dr Moshe Katz of the Haifa Technion made an impressive discovery. They used high-speed computers to analyse the first five books of the Bible, or 'Pentateuch'. The Law of Moses is known as the Torah. Now, the Hebrew language has no vowels, so the word 'Torah' is

The Make up of the Bible

represented by the four letters, TORH ('o' is not considered to be a vowel in Hebrew!). These men noticed that, starting with the first 'T' in Genesis, 50 letters on came 'O'; a further 50 letters brought 'R'; and the fiftieth next letter was 'H'. This fifty-letter sequence was repeated throughout the 50 chapters of the Book of Genesis: TORH, TORH, TORH ...

This same pattern was discovered in the 40 chapters of Exodus. However, the men were disappointed to find no such sequence in Leviticus. When they came to Numbers, however, they discovered the sequence was reversed. The fifty-letter gaps spelled out H R O T or 'Torah' in reverse. After ignoring the first five verses of Deuteronomy (which are taken from the Talmud), the same reverse sequence of H R O T was found.

So, what happened with Leviticus? When the men made a new study of this book, they found that the letters Y H W H (the Jewish holy name of God, Yahweh) is repeated throughout, this time at intervals of seven letters. A pattern has been forming:

Genesis	Exodus	Leviticus	Numbers	Deuteronomy
TORH	TORH	YHWH	HROT	HROT

God (YHWH) is at the centre of the Pentateuch. The Torah points towards YHWH from Genesis. It also points toward YHWH backwards from Deuteronomy. God is indeed at the heart of His Word! The scribes taking down Moses' words could not possibly have arranged these Hebrew letters in such an incredible way!

"All Scripture is God-breathed and is useful for teaching, rebuking, correcting and training in righteousness, so that the man of God may be thoroughly equipped for every good work."

(2 Tim 3: 16-17)

"Ask and it will be given to you;
seek and you will find;
knock and the door will be opened to you.
For everyone who asks receives;
he who seeks finds;
and to him who knocks,
the door will be opened."

(Matt 7: 7-8)

Section Four

Our Approach to the Word

If the Word of God is to be your constant companion, you should ensure that your copy is the one most suited to your needs. There is now such a wide range of different versions that selecting one may prove to be quite an ordeal. Choosing a Bible is rather like buying a pair of shoes: you need to be sure that you are comfortable with your choice. Happily, there are many Bibles these days that are a joy to look at – Bibles that have their text attractively laid out. To me, this is important. When buying a Bible, you should ensure that it is a pleasure to open its pages, as you could be doing so every day for the rest of your life!

Many homes will have a dusty King James Authorised Version on their shelves, the one I call the 'thee and thou' version, written in seventeenth-century English. You may be able to follow the familiar Gospel section, but when you come to other parts, you may struggle with the language. Take Philippians 1: 22 for example: *"... this is the fruit of my labour, yet what I choose I wot not."* Now, if that is perfectly clear, fine. If not, you might want to consider a modern translation.

Although all versions of the Bible are paraphrases to some extent, one or two versions have been paraphrased far more

SECTION 4

than the rest. The Good News Bible and the Living Bible are the best examples of these; they are certainly very popular. I do feel that they tend to make the Word of God somewhat subjective in the hands of those paraphrasing. Matthew 15: 31 in the Living Bible is a case in point, where the translators may have gone beyond the content of the original Word: *" ... And those with missing arms and legs had new ones."* Now, I do not doubt for a minute that our Lord could replace or provide legs that had been amputated or missing from birth; I just doubt if this is written in the Word of God. A literal translation from the Greek gives it as: "so as the crowd to marvel seeing dumb men speaking, maimed whole and lame walking and blind seeing".

The Amplified Bible is very concerned to give the full flavour of the original language by giving a number of words where they feel that one English word does not on its own quite match that of the source. I find this to be a very useful tool. However, it may prove difficult to read through smoothly with its many brackets and parentheses.

The New International Version (NIV) – probably the most popular these days – is an example of a well laid out, attractive Bible. This could perhaps be viewed as a first choice, because it is closer to the original texts than some of the others.. Having said that, it's important to stress that all of the versions discussed above, together with many others (such as the New American Standard Version, the Revised Standard Version, the New King James Version and the New English Bible) are the Word of God – all are brought to life through God's Holy Spirit. Which version is best suited to you is a matter of personal preference.

As a postscript to this subject, I would like to recommend the Scofield Study Bible as a useful tool. I am not a dispensationalist: I don't fully agree with all of their conclusions. Nevertheless, I find much to be learnt from C I

Scofield's writings. You know, there is a tendency for Christians to – as people used to say – 'throw out the baby with the bathwater'. I'm still capable of doing this. In a shop, I always test the book that I'm thinking of buying. I might flick through a work and become increasingly impressed with it. I might grow quite excited about how it could be a help to my spiritual worship. I would be about to go to the checkout, when I might spot a passage that says something like, "... and there it was that I had my first vision of Our Blessed Lady" – the book would then go straight back onto the shelf!

There is only one infallible book, and there is only one infallible Person. Why do some people expect a popular and well-used evangelist to be a perfect theologian? I see people on Internet sites decrying much-loved and much-used servants of God simply because they disagree on an aspect of predestination! There are basic doctrines on which we all should agree: We should all agree about the Fall of mankind; we should agree about the truth of Scripture. There should be no arguments against the fact that salvation is by faith alone, nor about the divinity of Christ and the three Persons of the Holy Trinity. Surely we should tolerate disagreements on lesser doctrines, those that do not have a bearing on our eternal position in our Lord?

However, we must never place any person on a pedestal; he or she is bound to fall off! Famous Christians need our prayers more than ordinary folk. Such people are certain to encounter massive attacks and many temptations from within the spiritual atmosphere. May God protect and guide us all on our spiritual journey!

Yes, there is only one infallible book. So, once you have chosen your Bible, how do you best go about reading it? Some feel that they should read it from cover to cover in order to get

---

① The publisher believes that the Bible is true, but not infallible.

SECTION 4

an overview before beginning specific studies. I do not share that view. In fact, not many who try this get past Leviticus before they give up! I strongly suggest that, except for the Psalms and possibly the Proverbs, new Christians should spend most of their time in the New Testament. They could start with the Gospels, and then perhaps move on to the Acts of the Apostles. The Old Testament could be initially approached when directed there by a cross-reference in the New Testament.

How much time to devote to Bible reading will vary from person to person, according to individual circumstances. Reading one chapter a day is more than enough. Reading just over three chapters a day will cover the whole Bible in a year, but there is no hurry. We should not bite off more than we can chew: each verse should be properly digested. However, we do need our daily nourishment; Satan would have us starve! John Bunyan warns us that either "Sin will keep you from this book, or this book will keep you from sin." A W Tozer adds, "Whatever keeps me from my Bible is my enemy, however harmless it may appear." J C Ryle urges: "We must read our Bibles like men digging for buried treasure."

Will you not open your heart to God's Word? Your Heavenly Father has eagerly waited for this day! He has so much that He wants to say to you; so much that He wants to teach you. Yes, you should always approach God's Word expecting to be taught, expecting to be spiritually fed. It is vitally important that we approach each portion of the Word as though we are seeing it for the first time. We must bring no preconceptions with us, no matter how many times we may have previously read or heard the passage before us.

Reading your Bible is as much an act of faith as praying. You should read it with your heart, not just your mind. What does that mean? Well, when I cast my mind back to my dreamy teenage years, when I think how I reacted to my first love letters; I didn't read those solely with my mind. You

Our Approach to the Word

know the sort of thing:
"I can't stop thinking about you", said the letter.
"She can't stop thinking about me," I repeated (over and over again).
"I can't wait until we next meet", continued the letter.
"She can't wait until we next meet," I digested – as if infusing each syllable into my bloodstream, as if introducing each word into the pores of my skin! So it should be for you when you read your Father's letter, for that is what the Bible is: your Father writing to you. When God's Word tells you of His love and concern for you, you must allow this into your heart; otherwise these precious words will simply be more theory.

You should also remember that, while God is talking to you in His Word, He is not always talking about you. For example, if you belong to Jesus, and God is telling you of His disappointment at those who will not trust Jesus; you should not take it personally. You will know when God is making a point to you. Text highlighters are not a recent discovery: Christians have been noticing them in the Word for centuries!

You should always be open to God's guidance concerning the subject matter for study. He is most eager to oversee your reading. Even in the middle of a lengthy study, you should always be prepared to stop and enquire whether God has another passage that He would have you read. There will be times when your private Bible study will be augmented by sermons or corporate studies in fellowship. A passage that you are currently studying at home will often be the subject under discussion in church. This is no coincidence: God is co-ordinating your development.

You should not approach the Bible as one would a ouija board. The following humorous example has become something of an old chestnut, one that you will probably have heard before: Someone opens the Bible, and, closing his eyes, he decides that the verse where his finger lands is his word

SECTION 4

from God for the day. Round and round in the air goes the finger, down it comes; the verse reads: *"Judas hanged himself"*. Not happy with that, he tries again. Down comes the finger on another page; the new verse reads: *"Go and do likewise"*! Having reminded you of that story, you should realise that there will sometimes be occasions when the Holy Spirit wants you to notice where you happen to have opened your Bible.

It is not sacrilegious to write in or mark your Bible. Many people do this. They find that these indications of where the Word has spoken to them in the past help confirm that their Bible is their personal living Word.

At this point, let us remember F B Meyer's important words: "Devout meditation on the Word is more important to soul-health even than prayer. It is more needful for you to hear God's Word than that God should hear yours, though the one will always lead to the other."

However, some parts of the Old Testament consist of long lists of names from the results of census counts. Elsewhere, the measurements of the tabernacle are repeated in intricate detail. Obviously, you must adjust your style of reading for these sections. You can at such points reflect on the fact that absolutely everything was noted and written down, and no doubt still is in the heavenly chronicles regarding the Church today and its activities.

You should never approach the Bible intent on proving a theory, because you probably will prove it – incorrectly! You should not read any Bible verse in isolation. You should see that verse in its context, and you should see that context as it sits within the whole of God's Word. Over the sixty-six books of Scripture, you will detect an amazing unity, and that unity is apparent despite the many different hands and hearts that God has used to bring His Word into being. Just as His Word has been given to us through those who have trusted God and been open to His Holy Spirit, so does His Word come to life in those

Our Approach to the Word

who are open to receive from Him. We step out in faith by placing our hearts into the middle of an ongoing two-way process. During this process faith is gained by reading the Word of God, and yet we only receive God's Word into our hearts as a result of that faith in Jesus that the Bible gives! This living Word is made accessible to us through Jesus' life-giving Spirit, the ultimate author of Scripture.

We must therefore "Pause at every verse of Scripture and shake, as it were, every bough of it, so that if possible some fruit at least might drop down." (Martin Luther)

Therefore, you should enjoy your studies and never think of them as a duty or penance. You should believe the Word, giving God the benefit of any doubt. You should also give God the opportunity to prove His Word by living your precious life in obedience to it.

The examples of Bible study in the following sections show the way that I approach God's Word. However, I certainly don't claim to have wrung the last ounce of meaning from the verses studied!

Prayer: *Heavenly Father, thank You for my Bible. Please give me a real hunger and thirst for Your Word. Help me to study it in a way that pleases You, so that it becomes an important part of my daily life – my daily life with You, Lord. I ask this in Jesus' holy name. Amen.*

"What are you doing here, Elijah?"
(1 Kings 19: 9)

"Where, O death, is your victory?
Where, O death, is your sting?"
(1 Cor 15: 55)

Section Five

Example Bible Study 1
Old Testament: 'History'

A Study of 1 Kings 19: 1-13

As previously pointed out, when we study the Old Testament 'History' section of the Bible, we tend to learn more from events that happened than from things that are said. We can see images of Jesus in the lives and actions of the people involved in the unfolding of God's plan. God is in control, despite the fact that there are often signs that would seem to dispute this. Just as God speaks to us through His Holy Spirit, so He also speaks to us through the circumstances in which He places us.

I strongly believe that each section of the Bible is as meaningful to us now as it was to the contemporaries of the events under discussion. I also strongly believe that the Bible is self-contained: it does not need us to have any other information for the words to have the desired effect on us. While those historically minded may find that background period details are of interest, I am convinced they are not necessary in order for us to understand what God is saying to us

SECTION 5

today. Because of this, I shall not fill out my comments with any historical details that are not already in the Bible.

Nothing in God's Word is superfluous. If something is mentioned just once, we should notice it. If something is repeated, it is because it is so important to our Father.

The chapter we are going to look at follows some of the greatest exhibitions of faith recorded in Scripture. We shall be looking at Elijah. The evil prophets of Baal had been utterly defeated, shown-up and executed and, in spite of all the signs to the contrary, Elijah had successfully predicted much-needed rainfall. One would have expected the prophet to be full of joy in the Lord after this success. Instead, we open our study to find him utterly downcast.

I recommend that the passage be read through now in order to obtain an overall picture. However, before studying any part of the Bible, we need to commit our study to the Lord. We need to ask for the help and guidance of the Holy Spirit, who is the ultimate author of all Scripture.

Prayer: *Heavenly Father, please speak to me now through Your Holy Word. Please help me to take it to my heart and into my life. I ask this in Jesus' name. Amen.*

Verses 1 and 2 give us the reason for Elijah's despondency. Ahab had told his wife Jezebel all that Elijah had done. Jezebel then sent a message to the prophet. She was obviously undeterred by the reported events, for she told Elijah that she would have him killed because he had killed her prophets. We can also see that, in spite of everything that had happened, Jezebel still relied on her gods. Some people are simply never going to believe; they blind themselves to the truth, no matter how many signs are given to them. Considering all that he had achieved, why did one woman have such an affect on Elijah?

Example Bible Study 1

Verse 3 tells us that he was afraid. How could this be? Tiredness could have been a factor. Anyone who has been involved in spiritual duties, such as healing, will know that, no matter how successful the service might have been, one is often physically drained afterwards. Jesus felt power leave Him when the sick woman touched His garment (Mark 5: 30). Many of us are also prone to concentrate on our failings, even when "our" successes far outweigh them. We are forgetting that they are actually God's successes. Elijah felt that he was no better than his ancestors were (v 4). How could Jezebel not believe, after such evidence of God's power? How could she still swear by her gods? Why does she want to kill me?

Often after a success, we transform our faith in God into a subtle belief in ourselves: a belief in our ability to believe. This belief then lets us down. Of course it will! Our Father must allow us to learn from this. Leaving his servant, perhaps to spare him from any harm, Elijah ran for his life ... he ran for his life! When God tells us to move, we must move. If we move on our own initiative, God will wait until we realise that we have left something behind: namely, our trust in Him!

After a day's journey into the desert, Elijah sits under a tree and prays for death. He has had enough (v 4). We don't know what had filled his mind on this day's journey. The fate of other prophets who had been slain had been considered. He feels that he is not good enough to escape a similar death. Maybe he feels that eluding physical death is the ultimate sign of God's favour, and that the earlier prophets had somehow failed.

Death and the thought of death have amazing power over the soulish mind (1 Cor 15: 56); it is Satan's greatest weapon. Under his tree, Elijah prays. He wants God to take his life, not Satan. He is not necessarily suicidal; he is placing himself in God's hands. The Lord gives him sleep (v 5). In our despair, the Lord will give a haven and refreshment. Verse 6 shows us that God supernaturally provided for Elijah via an angel. He

SECTION 5

will do the same for us, if our situation requires it. *"I was young and now I am old, yet I have never seen the righteous forsaken or their children begging bread"* (Psalm 37: 25).

God had made provision for Elijah, but He had not yet addressed him on recent events. God had made provision through an angel. I am not now entering into a discourse on angels, but they certainly do exist. I am sure that most Christians will encounter an angel at least once on their journey through life, although they may not realise that they have been assisted in this way (Heb 13: 2).

There is an important difference in verse 7. The angel is now referred to as *"the angel of the Lord"*. Jesus is often 'the' (as opposed to 'an') Angel of the Lord. Let's think about this: Elijah was unhappy with the world, he was disillusioned with himself and he had asked God to take his life. He was then looked after by Jesus. Isn't this exactly what happens to us, when we give up our lives to God!

Elijah is then strengthened; he travels forty days and nights, until he reaches the mountain of God (v 8). He enters a cave and there he spends the night (v 9). Elijah thus had forty days and nights in which to reflect on what had happened. Although too much can be made of this, numbers are significant in the Bible. Very briefly and selectively:

1   The number of God
2   The number of union and fellowship
3   The number of God expressed or perfected
4   The number of created things
6   The number of man – on its own, it represents fallen man or Satan
7   The number of earthly perfection (four, the created, plus three, God)
10 The number of fallen or worldly completeness (four plus six)

Example Bible Study 1

12 The number of heavenly perfection (four multiplied by or compounded by 3)

So forty days and nights indicate the period of worldly completeness necessary for created man to endure (ten multiplied by or compounded by four). We could compare Moses' forty years in the wilderness or the four hundred-year wait for a Word from God, following the final "history" book. Some people treat noughts representing hundreds or thousands as emphasising exclamation marks. Hence: 400, to them, is 40! 4000 would be 40!! Now, if all this seems like so much nonsense, I would reiterate, too much can be read into such ideas.

After forty days and nights, Elijah reaches the mountain of God. He enters a cave and spends the night there. Then, at the second part of verse 9, we have that wonderful word from God, *"What are you doing here, Elijah?"*

This really is wonderful!

We can read this on two levels. Firstly, Elijah had wanted to escape. He ran away. Then, when he feels he is all alone, the Lord says to him, *"What are you doing here, Elijah?"* It is as if to say, "I am everywhere. You have travelled and wearied yourself, and yet I am everywhere you are. I was with you in the valleys and I am with you on the mountain. I was with you in trouble and I am with you in calm." Where indeed can we go from the Lord!

The second and more profound meaning emphasises the "you". "What are *you* doing here, Elijah?" This was the mountain of the Law (Sinai / Horeb). This was the mountain that Moses had ascended in order to get the Ten Commandments (Exod 19: 20). Elijah was symbolic of something greater than the Law: he was to symbolise faith in the promise of God. As such, this mountain was not

SECTION 5

appropriate for Elijah: "What are *you* doing here?"

Verse 10 gives Elijah's response. He has been zealous for God; he has been concerned that God's people had rejected their Lord. He feels that he is the only one remaining who is prepared to be obedient to God. He feels that, as a result, his days are numbered. Now, whereas God had told Moses, who symbolises the Law, to hide in a kind of cave when the presence of God passed by (Exod 33: 21-23), Elijah is now told (v 11a) to stand on the mountain. Those who have known Jesus are prepared to meet with God Himself, and not merely His Word impressed on stone. We are not expected to simply choose Jesus in blind faith so that, when we die, we will say, "Oh good, I made the right choice!" When we commit our lives to Jesus, we can know the presence of God as a regular deposit on our heavenly inheritance.

Verses 11b-13 teach us even more. Elijah is told to expect the Lord's presence. Three strange phenomena then occur: strong wind, earthquake and fire. When we think about this, is it not typical! We become a Christian, expecting peace and freedom from worry; instead, we get problems: we are shaken and things are destroyed. We are about to despair; we are about to give up, when a still small voice, a gentle whisper has us in awe (v 13). We used to belong to Satan by default. When we were his, he was happy to leave us alone. But when we became spiritual, when we gave our lives to Jesus, when we start causing great cosmic upheaval through our believing prayers, then Satan doesn't like it. We withstand all Satan's efforts, and then he will flee from us (James 4: 7). We can then hear God's still voice, and we learn that in Jesus we can indeed be free from worry.

Example Bible Study 1

Unlike Satan, God does not nag. Unlike Satan, God does not shout – He doesn't have to. A favourite hymn has the last verse:

> Breathe through the heats of our desire
> Thy coolness and Thy balm;
> Let sense be dumb, let flesh retire;
> Speak through the earthquake, wind and fire,
> O still, small voice of calm!
>
> (J G Whittier)

Elijah is again in a position to be used by God. He is reassured by the fact that the Lord has reserved for Himself seven thousand (number!) who had not bowed their heads to Baal. The chapter finishes with God's call of Elisha into service. God has chosen him to take Elijah's place. Elisha is not on his knees waiting for God's special spiritual call; he is busy working in the fields. But rather like the fishermen who were to abandon their nets in order to become fishers of men, Elisha was to sow seed for God after burning his plough.

Elijah does not see death after all! After handing over the prophetic mantle to Elisha, he is carried up into heaven (2 Kings 2: 11). He is alive. On another mountain, we see him with Jesus. He was with our Lord on the Mount of Transfiguration (Matt 17: 1-3).

Praise the Lord!

"I will counsel you and watch over you"
(Psalm 32: 8)

"Rejoice in the Lord always.
I will say it again: Rejoice!"
(Phil 4: 4)

Section Six

Example Bible Study 2
Old Testament: 'Poetry'

A Study of Psalm 32

Out from all the wonderful writings contained within the Old Testament 'poetry' section, the Psalms shine like a diamond. Just what it is that makes the Psalms so deeply and movingly special is difficult to define. Many simply see them as an old hymnbook. It's true that some contain musical instructions, and were therefore sung in assembly; but there is more to the Psalms than that, much more. We all have our favourite hymns and choruses that move us towards a more efficient and meaningful worship, but the Psalms somehow hit an even deeper spot.

Jesus quoted more from the Psalms than from any other source in Scripture. Although David penned most of them, there are a number of other contributors. The Psalms are a part of the Word of God; we must therefore credit the Holy Spirit with their authorship. We saw in Book 1 that the Holy Spirit offers up prayers on our behalf from within our human spirits,

SECTION 6

prayers about which we know nothing. Well, we surely have here examples of perfect prayers, as well as examples of perfect worship – such as takes place in Heaven!

Some psalms are called 'Messianic'; this means that they give us a portrait of Jesus. Psalm 22, for example, gives a very vivid picture of Jesus on the cross.

Some are concerned when the psalmist wishes ill on his adversaries; they feel that this is not compatible with "turning the other cheek". I see these sections as prophecies, not curses. Here David is the mouthpiece of God; these words confirm the fact that God will avenge for the righteous. We also notice psalms in which David is asking why God has abandoned him. This shows that it is perfectly in order to call on God and question Him out of our own distress, when we too feel that we are all alone.

Let's now begin our study of Psalm 32. Once we have read the psalm through, we should approach our Father in prayer, asking Him to bless our study of it:

Prayer: *Heavenly Father, help me to be open to Your Word. In it may I see You as my protector, and then let me sing Your praises. Let me sing from a heart that is turned towards You. I ask this in Jesus' holy name. Amen.*

Many of us know the relief that is felt when a burden is lifted from our chest. A problem shared is a problem halved, some say. This psalm offers us far more than a halved problem. God has promised not only to forgive us, but that He will also cast all memory of our sins from His sight. Verse 1 uses the word 'covered'. Our sins are covered by the huge payment that Jesus made for us at Calvary. 'Covered' also conveys the picture of our sins being hidden; they are out of sight.

Example Bible Study 2

Verse 2 speaks of a human spirit without deceit. The Bible tells us that the human heart is deceitful above all things (Jer 17: 9). Just who were we deceiving? It certainly wasn't God. How heavy does deceit weigh on our hearts, and how cunning was the sin that brought deceit! How deceitful was Satan, who tried to convince us that we were inseparable from our sins. How heavy indeed does all this weigh! Bones wasting, groaning all day, strength sapped; these are all figures of our discomfort. They are the price that we were prepared to pay for our sin. All the time our Father waited for us to break our silence with Him. Indeed, these verses tell us that some of our discomforts were the result of the Lord's prodding.

"Selah" ... This probably means, 'pause here and reflect'. We must be in no hurry when the Lord is moving our hearts. If the Lord tells us to pause, it could well mean that He is prepared to speak to us at this point. Let's be quiet for a moment now in order that the Lord can impress His will upon our hearts ... Selah.

The sun comes out in verse 5. *"Then I acknowledged my sin to You"*. We no longer cover up our iniquity. What caused us to confess? Certainly, the pressure of deceit could have become unbearable. The Word of God may have warned our hearts, or a friend may have spoken of God's love for us. Something had to give: often, it is our pride. In every transaction, there is a price; if not money, perhaps it's time. If not time, perhaps it's the giving up of an alternative activity. We give up our sin for God's peace. We abandon our inflated egos in favour of Jesus Christ.

For the psalmist, this was in the past, as no doubt it is for many of us. We lived with our sins. Eventually we took them to the cross of the Lord, and that was an end to them. As soon as we realise that we have succumbed to further sinning, we take this to the Lord in repentance. The Lord is faithful and

SECTION 6

true to His Word, and we receive His forgiveness once again (1 John 1: 9).

In verses 1-5, David remembers and recounts his Father's kindness to him. God, in turn, is pleased to listen. All parents enjoy looking back over their child's progress; they love retelling old stories of former times, much to the child's embarrassment! God would have been pleased to hear David's estimation of just how far he had come under His Lord's guidance. Except in an emergency, our prayers should not begin with our requests: we should first enjoy the Lord's presence.

Remembering God's kindness fuelled David's faith. He can now move on and pray for others. Verse 6 has David asking God to allow others who are guilty to pray to Him. We too must pray for those who, as yet, don't know that God is ready and waiting with forgiveness.

Verse 6 also has a solemn truth in it. *"while You may be found"* indicates that there will be a time – probably the predicted 'Great Tribulation' – when the Holy Spirit will be withdrawn with the Church. *"when the mighty waters rise"* (v 6) supports this feeling of a future destruction. This is figurative, as God has promised never again to use a flood to achieve His ends (Gen 9: 11); but there will be a tribulation. Verse 6 tells us that this shall not affect those whose sins are forgiven. What a call to prayer this is! God is available now and He is open for business! Verse 7 continues this. God is now our hiding place. There will be no hiding place on earth when all this destruction happens. Christians are protected from trouble; they will be with the Lord amid *"songs of deliverance"*.

Something wonderful happens next! Often during our prayers, the Lord will address our hearts. At such times, we know that our prayers are answered and our faith is fuelled.

Example Bible Study 2

God always answers faithful prayers. Sometimes the answer is "no" or "not yet", but there is always an answer. Verse 8 shows the Lord's fatherly love for His children. "I will instruct you, teach you, counsel you and watch over you." Let's stop and allow our hearts to be filled with these great words. Let's take time to wallow in the fact that this is God's Holy Word promising that He will watch over us, that He will teach us. How hard it is to leave verse 8. We should abide here for a while ...

Verse 9 is God's word for David, David's reward for his prayer. It's also for us. "Don't be like a horse or a mule." How many of us are like a horse? We think we know what our Father wants – and off we go! We charge off without waiting for the Lord, without thinking of the consequences of our actions or seeking confirmation that it's what God wants. I wonder how many people have taken up some huge project or removed themselves to some far corner of the world – things that God has neither asked them nor equipped them to do. As verse 9 says: we are without understanding. It's as if we are telling Jesus to follow us. If God does not somehow restrain us, we will not come back to Him. Our pride must be checked.

On the other hand, are we like a mule? Nothing will get us started: "No, not me Lord; I'm far too shy. Other people find this kind of thing much easier than I do. And besides, You know I have a special weakness". Are we stubborn, untrustworthy and unreliable? Here, the bit and brace are used to pull us into action. Jesus rode on a donkey during His triumphant entry into Jerusalem. The donkey doesn't charge ahead, nor is it unmoving as a mule can be. The donkey made Jesus approachable and accessible.

Refreshed and renewed from his prayer, David can bolster his heart and ours with his summary (vv 10-11): many are the woes of the wicked, but the Lord's unfailing love surrounds

SECTION 6

those who trust in Him. Yes, God's love surrounds us. His love goes ahead of us into tomorrow; it is also behind us: screening us from Satan and our sin.

What should we do now? What else can we do? Verse 11 tells us to sing, rejoice and be glad. So many psalms end with a call to praise, no matter what the situation. Praising God is both a tonic and an antidote to Satan's efforts. The Lord loves our sincere praise – Satan hates it!

> Praise, my soul, the King of heaven,
> To His feet thy tribute bring;
> Ransomed, healed, restored, forgiven,
> Who like thee His praise should sing?
> Alleluia! Alleluia!
> Praise the everlasting King!
>
> (H F Lyte)

Praise Him, indeed!

The people of a village were holding their gala talent show. The last act had just begun. Saul was reciting the twenty-third psalm. In a wonderful Richard Burton-type voice, he was eloquently enunciating each verse. At that point, Paul arrived. He had recently recovered from a life-threatening sickness, but he was determined to take part in the proceedings.

"Am I too late?" he asked.

"The last act is on now, but I expect we can fit you in. What would you like to do?"

Paul didn't need to think about this: "I must recite the twenty-third psalm."

"Oh dear, somebody is reciting that as we speak; still I don't suppose it would matter if you were to do the same. You go on after Saul."

Saul rounded off his recital, and when he had finished, the hall broke out in loud, spontaneous cheers and applause.

On walked Paul. He did not have the strong, rich-toned voice that Saul had. In fact, his voice was trembling, and his hands could be seen to shake. He recited the psalm. When he finished, there was not the applause and cheering that Saul had received, but there was not a dry eye in the hall!

Later, at the bar, two friends were summing up the evening:

"It was strange that they let two people recite the same thing. The first one really knew that psalm."

"Yes," said his friend, "but the second one knew the Shepherd!"

" 'There is no peace,' says my God, 'for the wicked'."

(Isaiah 57: 21)

"When a farmer ploughs for planting, does he plough continually?
Does he keep on breaking up and harrowing the soil?"

(Isaiah 28: 24)

Section Seven

Example Bible Study 3
Old Testament: 'Prophets'

A Study of Isaiah 57: 14 - 21

I have already mentioned some aspects of prophecy. We briefly discussed the fact that these spiritual messages need not be complete or in order. We saw that a single message can be a reference to more than one forthcoming event. I have also mentioned that to prophesy means to speak forth God's word, and that this does not necessarily refer to future events.

Prophets such as Isaiah were very special people. It is difficult for us in this Church age to fully appreciate this. We, as members of the Body of Christ, not only have the Holy Spirit indwelling our human spirits; we can also receive the anointing or outpouring of the Holy Spirit such as the Old Testament prophets received. Isaiah was writing under such an anointing. The prophet was given spiritual eyes so that he could see the message of God. The descriptive words used by the prophet were probably his: I don't think of prophets as being merely dictating machines.

SECTION 7

Ezekiel gave us some very colourful images of the scene around the throne of God. Visions such as this had to be described in words that would mean something to us. I doubt that the earth has glories to compare with the heavenly splendour that was shown to Ezekiel. The prophet had to do the best he could when trying to describe what he saw. Someone once gave me a mental picture of a desert island, one that has not yet been visited by man. A 'prophet' crab was given a vision of man's impending arrival there. The prophet would have to describe man in such a way that the other crabs could identify with his words. He could only say that man had no shell and no pincers. Talk of hair, fingers and feet would have been meaningless to the other crabs. The hymn writer could only describe God as not mortal, not visible and that He is uniquely wise. Spiritual descriptions of God would be lost on us.

Let us now begin our chosen study from Isaiah.

Prayer: *Heavenly Father, please help me to understand Your prophetic Word. Grant that I may have eyes to see and a mind to absorb just what You are saying to me in this passage. I ask this in Jesus' holy name. Amen.*

Verse 14 begins, *"And it will be said, 'Build up, build up, prepare the road! Remove the obstacles out of the way of My people' "*
It was indeed said: by John the Baptist, when he called for people to repent and prepare a way for the Lord Jesus (Matt 3: 1-3). What are the obstacles to be removed? We shall see that pride is one of the first things to be taken away. However, perhaps the main obstacle referred to here is the Law that condemns us. Jesus died to free us from the Law (Rom 8: 1-4).

Verse 16 seems to confirm this, as God says here that He will not accuse us forever.

"God is high and lofty." Some people are not quite happy when the Bible reports Almighty God, our Lord Jesus or apostles such as Paul appearing to 'blow their own trumpet'. I used to think Paul extremely arrogant – not any more! We should not avoid the truth by seeking and showing false modesty. How can God be modest? Human modesty arrives out of our deep-rooted awareness of sin. When we have been rid of sin because of Jesus Christ, we can say quite confidently that we are saved and that we are going to heaven. It isn't boasting; it's a fact. People who feel safer saying that they hope to go to heaven, people who dare not speak of their heavenly inheritance are simply displaying a lack of assurance.

God lives forever. His name is holy and He lives in a holy place (v 15). How unsuitable would heaven be for sinners, those not made holy by God! However, we are not sanctified in a moment. Unlike our salvation, which is instant, it can take a lifetime to be made holy: a lifetime of closeness to God and His Word. Our lives before our regeneration were a pale shadow of the lives that God had planned for us. We were steeped in sin. We had built up our own characters by imitating fallen, worldly personality traits that had impressed us. We moved further and further away from the people that God wanted us to be. We were living a lie. All this had to be put to death. Yes, we were saved the moment we believed in Jesus; at that time, we received our new lives. We are now being made more holy each day as we develop these new lives in Jesus. God can at last begin to use us, and we can now be the characters that He had created us to be.

Not only does God live in a high and holy place, He also lives in the hearts of His children, through His Holy Spirit. There is a condition, though: God cannot live in a proud or haughty heart. In such a heart, there is no room for Him!

SECTION 7

Notice that even in Old Testament times, God promises to be "with" those who are contrite and lowly in spirit (v 15). Only since the outpouring of His Spirit at Pentecost can we have His indwelling life.

"To revive the spirit of the lowly and the heart of the contrite" (v 15); this carries on the subject of "God lives". God lives to revive our spirits and our hearts if we are not proud – if we are repentant and aware of the mire from which we have been lifted. God is active in this. Those who have an image of Almighty God leaning back on His throne are here proved wrong. Jesus said, *"My Father is always at His work to this very day"* (John 5: 17), and here we see that a part of this work is revival. Verses 18 and 19 both speak of God being active in healing.

God will not accuse forever (v 16). God will not always be angry. God never holds us responsible for the fact that there is sin in the world; He only notes our response to sin. The Lord knows that the man He created by His breath would grow faint under too much pressure. The ploughing should only last for a season: then the seed can go in. Are we ready for the seed?

Greed, resulting in wilful ways, is the thing next highlighted (v 17). God does punish us and He can seem to be absent from us at times. We have two options: we can be stubborn and turn our backs, or we can be repentant; only the latter restores God to our hearts. Then we can apply the precious verse 18 to ourselves. Then God "notices us"; He heals us, guides us and we receive comfort from Him as our Father.

We should never hold some kind of modernistic, new age thought that God 'winks' at sin, rather like those parents who say that they wouldn't want completely obedient children. God never gets that anyway; we should not worry on His behalf on

that score!
    What is the result of our trust in God? We praise Him. Verse 19 tells us that God creates His own praise on the lips of mourners (those truly sorry), and that He gives us peace. There is only one place from which to obtain peace, and that is from God. Peace to those far and near: God's peace will not be restricted to the Israelites: it will also be for the Gentiles – for you and me.

Verse 20 gives us another warning: The wicked cannot receive God's peace. Those who are blown about by this world's false pleasures, climbing on one social or religious bandwagon after another; uncertain, unbelieving, never resting, never still; God's silence would be an abomination to them, all silence is. How Satan and the world love to rob us of our times of quiet reflection! How Satan hates us being still and knowing God! Mobile phones and personal stereos now blight public transport journeys. Bars and cafés are awash with the sounds of gaming machines. Booming base-driven car stereos from passing vehicles or music playing loudly through open windows often interrupt a peaceful quiet time in our gardens.
    I have to admit that I used to be addicted to music. The first thing I would do after arriving home would be to turn on some music. Silence was repulsive to me. And yes, I must also admit that I was one of the worst offenders in respect of playing my music loudly through an open window! I still enjoy my music, including rock music, but it is no longer a compulsion for me. I know now that long periods of quiet are beneficial to my spiritual well-being. Many people are now driven by instant gratification. 'Must have' products and brand labels are treated as an indispensable part of modern life. All of this Satan promotes with relish. No, there is no peace for the wicked (v 21). Peace and quiet is now for many people simply unbearable; spiritual reflection has become almost impossible

SECTION 7

for them. The result, says God's Word, is 'mire and mud'.

Someone once described us all as being like fish, swimming in a muddy, filthy tank. Next to our dirty tank was another one with crystal-clear water. Jesus wants to cup His hands and gently lift us from the filthy tank. He wants to place us into the tank of pure water, with fresh whatever-it-is that fish like to eat. We at first say, no. We are used to our filthy tank. We are not at all sure that we would like it where all things are clean and pure. But when we finally give Jesus permission to move us ... how wonderful it is!

"*Grace and peace to you from God our Father and from the Lord Jesus Christ*"

(Rom 1:7b)

"My grace is sufficient for you"

(2 Cor 12: 9)

Section Eight

Grace and Peace

Our studies now bring us to the New Testament. Before the next Bible study, I want to underline the point that, except for the Gospels, the New Testament was written solely for committed Christians. The greater part of the New Testament is there to develop disciples for Jesus; it is written to those who have already accepted Jesus as their Lord. The Gospels are different: they are the evangelist's seed. We should make sure as many people as possible hear the Gospel of Jesus Christ. As Paul puts it, milk is for new infant Christians, who, on their rebirth, are literally babes in Christ. However, a part of Paul's letter to the Corinthians conveys his frustration with the Church there because they still wanted milk rather than the solid food that he wanted to feed them through his letters (1 Cor 3: 2). Yes, the letters were written exclusively for God's reborn disciples, in the hope that these disciples will progress from milk to solid food. It is therefore not surprising if non-Christians are unmoved by quotes from the teaching letters of Paul, as these words were specially given to spiritually nourish Christ's born again flock.

Hebrews adds, *"In fact, though by this time you ought to be teachers, you need someone to teach you elementary truths of*

SECTION 8

God's Word all over again. You need milk, not solid food! Anyone who lives on milk, being still an infant, is not acquainted with the teaching about righteousness. But solid food is for the mature, who by constant use have trained themselves to distinguish good from evil" (Heb 5: 12-14).

The Gospels are for everybody; the rest of the New Testament is for those who have given their lives to Jesus. It would be false teaching to read Philippians 4: 13, *"I can do everything through Him who gives me strength"*, to those not reborn in Jesus Christ, as these words are only applicable to disciples of Jesus. Like Mary on that Easter morning, Jesus must also tell us that we are no longer to cling to the physical image we have of Him; He is risen. The image of the risen Jesus given to us in Revelation is a far more regal one than that given to us in the Gospels. We are in fellowship with the spiritual, risen Christ. We are now spiritual beings, and as such we need spiritual food. Although we shall not completely outgrow our need for the Gospel Word in this life, we must have spiritual nourishment in order to grow as disciples.

Enquirers are told to *"stay in the city until you have been clothed with power from on high"* (Luke 24: 49). The power of the indwelling Holy Spirit is given when people open their hearts to Jesus. It is only after we have received this power that the epistles can speak to us. If we were to take a random look at the teaching letters, whether they are by Paul, Peter or John, they nearly all start with the words of blessing: "Grace and Peace". I see this not only as a wish, such as, "have a nice day", but also as an essential requirement. I see this as a kind of door. In order for us to go in and receive all of the solid food that these letters contain, we must have God's grace and His peace.

On pages 62-63 I have tabulated the New Testament letters and have indicated (G&P) where they contain this benediction or prayer for grace and peace. We can also see from the list that these letters were indeed addressed to committed Christians.

If you will allow that the Bible is saying that individually and corporately we need grace and peace from God, then how do we receive them? I believe that the order here is all-important. Grace comes before peace. We all know that grace is God bestowing unmerited blessings upon us; we can never deserve them, yet they are ours in Jesus Christ. Peace follows the receipt of God's grace. We enter the wisdom of the New Testament by the grace and peace of God. It is to be expected that all Christians have grace and peace. If we do not have peace, then something is wrong. If we do not have peace, then it follows that something is interfering with the supply of God's grace. What could cause such an obstruction?

Of course, our sins are a prime candidate – repeated sins about which our Father has been trying to talk to us. In such cases, we need to return to the Gospels. We need to return to the cross of Jesus and see just what God thinks of our sin. We also need to see just what He has done to our sin.

A lack of forgiveness for those who have hurt us causes a blockage in our channel for receiving from God. The Lord's Prayer points out that we can only receive God's grace, His forgiveness for our own sins, in the same measure that we forgive others. Our forgiveness must be an act of will, not a response to our feelings. We may never feel like forgiving somebody who has hurt us, but we must; it is vital. Many a miraculous healing has been given to people who have offered forgiveness where it was previously refused.

Pain and sickness understandably preoccupy the hearts and minds of many sufferers. Jesus had time for all who were sick. We live in a fallen world and sickness is just one result of this. The Gospels tell us that Jesus has overcome the world, and that we can now overcome it in Him.

SECTION 8

THE NEW TESTAMENT LETTERS

Book	By	G&P?	To whom addressed
Romans	Paul	G&P	All loved by God and called to be saints.
1 Corinth.	Paul	G&P	Those sanctified in Jesus and called to be holy.
2 Corinth.	Paul	G&P	Church and all the saints.
Galatians	Paul	G&P	Churches.
Ephesians	Paul	G&P	The saints, the faithful in Jesus.
Philippians	Paul	G&P	Saints in Jesus plus overseers and deacons.
Colossians	Paul	G&P	Holy and faithful brothers.
1 Thess.	Paul	G&P	Church in God the Father and Jesus Christ.
2 Thess.	Paul	G&P	Church in God the Father and Jesus Christ.
1 Timothy	Paul	G&P	True son in the faith.

Grace and Peace

Book	By	G&P?	To whom addressed
2 Timothy	Paul	G&P	Dear son.
Titus	Paul	G&P	True son in our common faith.
Philemon	Paul	G&P	Fellow worker, fellow soldier and House Church
Hebrews	?		Holy brethren who share in heavenly calling.
James	James		Brothers.
1 Peter	Peter	G&P	God's elect, strangers in the world.
2 Peter	Peter	G&P	Those who have received precious faith.
1 John	John		Children, young men, fathers in Christ.
2 John	John	G&P	Chosen lady.
3 John	John		Dear friend in the truth.
Jude	Jude	P	Those who have been called.
Revelation	John	G&P	Seven Churches.

SECTION 8

Are we still as excited about the Lord as we were when we first believed? Let's not delude ourselves by thinking that it is God's love that has grown cold!

Pride also causes a lack of peace. Those relying on self do not hand over the reigns easily. Such people must return to the Gospels and hear again our Lord's words – especially those that He said to the proud Pharisees.

Worry puts us in a position where we cannot hear the Lord. The Bible tells us that we have been raised into the heavens; we have access to the throne of God. However, we need to return to the Gospels and hear again our Lord telling us not to be anxious about anything (Matt 6: 25). Our spirits may well be with the Lord in the heavens, but so often our worrying minds are well and truly on the ground, inciting our hearts to follow our fears rather than our Lord.

Yes, a divided heart can often affect our peace. Some may be confused between the parts played by our souls and our hearts. In the first book, I said that the soul is where all of our decisions are made. This is true. However, I also said that the heart is the driving force of one's spirit, soul and body. The following scenario may help to show the difference:

My vicar telephones me at lunchtime on Saturday, saying that he would like me to attend an emergency meeting at the church. My soul needs to make a decision. My mind decides that it makes sense to attend. My emotions were not involved – unless, that is, the vicar was sobbing as he asked me! The decision was made: I agreed to attend, and at 3.30 pm I was duly at the meeting. My vicar seemed pleased to see me – but I could sense that God was not completely happy with me. You see, my heart was at Stamford Bridge Football Ground, wondering how Chelsea were getting on!

Let's now take the same situation, but with a different outcome: When the vicar telephones, I say that I agree that the

Grace and Peace

meeting is important, but I also add that I don't think that I could contribute anything of value, and conclude that I shall not be attending. At 3.00 pm, I am at home listening to the radio, and the Chelsea game is being broadcast. But something is wrong! Instead of enjoying the game, I feel disturbed. I have a lack of peace because my conscience is troubled. A message seems to arrive deep within me that my mind interprets as, "Dave, is this football game really more important than work for My Kingdom?" I grab my coat, and arrive at the meeting just before 3.30 pm. However, my heart is now completely focused on the meeting.

So what should have happened? Well, after agreeing to attend the meeting, and after realising that I would have to miss the football match, I should have brought it all before the Lord, confessing my divided heart. He could then give me His blessing and His word. This enables me to attend the meeting with a 'correctly tuned', peaceful heart. Now, there is absolutely nothing wrong with listening to a football match; it is simply a question of priorities. Do you see that, while the soul makes the decisions, the heart has a tremendous influence on those decisions? Through His Holy Spirit, God can address our hearts. Like the psalmist, we should regularly ask our Father to 'search our hearts'.

Despite our need to take in the solid spiritual food that the New Testament letters offer us, it must be obvious from the above that we never fully outgrow our need of the Gospels in this life. The Holy Spirit will often return us to Jesus' Gospel words – words that will *"never pass away"* (Matt 24: 35).

One final point on this subject: Peace does not necessarily mean 'peace and quiet'. Even when chaos reigns all around us, we can still enjoy the peace that Jesus gives. Jesus' peace is a quiet inner contentment that trusts in God even when there are signs all around us that seem to contradict that trust.

SECTION 8

Prayer: *Heavenly Father, please let nothing block the path of Your grace to me. Let nothing get in the way of Your peace. Lord, You grant me grace and peace as my natural inheritance – my natural inheritance in Jesus Christ, in whose name I thank You. Amen.*

"Blessed are the poor in spirit,
for theirs is the kingdom of heaven"
(Matt 5: 3)

"When Jesus had finished saying these things,
the crowds were amazed at His teaching,
because He taught as one who had authority"
(Matt 7: 28-29)

Section Nine

Example Bible Study 4
New Testament – Gospels

A Study of Matthew 5: 3-12

The Gospel portion that we are about to study is a sermon from Jesus initially addressed to His disciples (Matt 5: 1). It was obviously overheard by a great many people as Matthew (7: 28) tells us: *"When Jesus had finished sayings these things the crowds were amazed".*

I think it is fair to say that Jesus wanted to shock His hearers. He wanted to make an impact that would not be forgotten. He succeeded. He was disappointed, to say the least, at the religious leaders of the day, who were mainly concerned with the letter of the Law, and not with the spirit behind it. Not only did they seem ignorant of the spiritual depths of the Law, they seemed also to be ignorant of the love, mercy and compassion that the Law of God incorporated. Let's now look at Jesus' words.

Example Bible Study 4

Prayer: *Heavenly Father, Jesus' words live forever. May they be forever inscribed on my heart, so that I may know Him and follow Him more closely and more lovingly! I ask this in His name. Amen.*

"Blessed are the poor in spirit". Here Matthew adds the meaning that is missing from Luke's account (Luke 6: 20): *"Blessed are you who are poor ...."* Luke no doubt wanted to preserve the shock effect of Jesus' sermon. *"Blessed are the poor in spirit ..."* Here is the first shock. Blessed are the poor? That would certainly be a shock to the Jews! One thing that the Jews could not easily take on board is that one could be poor and blessed! But Jesus says that the poor shall inherit. *"... for theirs is the kingdom of heaven."* The poor shall inherit the kingdom about which Jesus preaches.

This is the first step on the Christian road; this is the first rung up the spiritual ladder; or, as I have seen illustrated, the first step up to the temple of God. We can start in no other way. We must be humble, or "poor in spirit". If we start with pride, we shall stumble. I don't think it an exaggeration to say that most Christians do not surmount this first hurdle. Yes, they are saved, and they will live forever. When people gives their lives to Jesus, God always takes them seriously – even many years on with little further involvement from them. We remain Christians unless we renounce Jesus. God will never give up on anybody; He strives for the attention of His children – even those who have forgotten the fact that they have a loving Heavenly Father. However, it's a sad fact that most baptism or confirmation candidates do not go on to become disciples, they remain babies in Christ.

But Jesus can teach the humble; He can build them up. Jesus cannot build up the proud; there is no room in their hearts left for Jesus to work in. The eyes of the proud are on their

SECTION 9

own advancement; the humble are happy to look at Jesus; He is sufficient for them.

Enter shock number two: blessed are those who mourn! Give Jesus the humble and He will turn mourning (v 4) into comfort. For the humble will now mourn the condition of the world. They will also mourn their own sinfulness. Jesus came for sinners. Yes, the humble now realise their sinfulness and mourn. Comfort comes from its only source: our Saviour Jesus Christ.

The next stage is meekness and patience (v 5). Another shock: it's the meek, not the pushy, the strong or the impatient who will inherit the earth. Meekness follows mourning. Jesus is teaching and training His disciples. What follows this meekness and long-suffering? It's a hunger and thirst for righteousness (v 6). What God's people have seen in Jesus, they now long for for themselves. And, yes, they will be filled. The righteousness of Jesus is ours. Having been given this righteousness, they will never forget from whence they came. They relied on the love and mercy of God, and they know that they must apply this same mercy (v 7) to their fellow men and women. They will obtain mercy for themselves in the same measure as they apply it, which must be liberal.

Where are you on this road? How far are you up the ladder? You may not realise it, but if you have reached this far, then you have a pure, unsullied heart (v 8). The Lord can see it. You, in turn, will see God: maybe not yet with your eyes, although one day you will. You shall see Him in His Word. You shall see Him through His Holy Spirit, and you shall see Him in the situations in which He places you. Yes, you shall see God all around you.

You are now in a position to make and maintain peace (v 9), for you are now a true vessel of Jesus. The peace for which you used to search can now come to others via you, as you are now a channel of God's love. What God has is yours;

Example Bible Study 4

what you have is His. God is unquestionably your Father; you are His son or daughter.

But there is a price. Jesus always warned us that there would be a price. You will be persecuted (v 10) for your faith, which is now so evident. *"All men will hate you because of Me. But not a hair of your head will perish. By standing firm you will gain life"* (Luke 21: 17-19). You are to count yourself blessed indeed, when your Christianity shows so much that it worries Satan. You will withstand the worst of Satan's attacks, and you will be able to bear it when proud, worldly people scoff at your faith.

So how far have you come? There are seven stages up the ladder before you are deemed worthy enough to share in the Lord's suffering. It all begins with humility, and ends with your being a son or daughter of God!

If being a Christian was a crime punishable by death, is there enough evidence around to convict you?

> "Put on the full armour of God
> so that you can take your stand
> against the devil's schemes"
>
> (Eph 6: 11)

> "... and the sword of the Spirit,
> which is the Word of God"
>
> (Eph 6: 17)

Section Ten

Example Bible Study 5
New Testament – Letters

A Study of Ephesians 6: 10-18

I have already mentioned quite a lot about the New Testament letters, especially the fact that they are written solely for Christians, those belonging to Jesus Christ. Let me also emphatically say that in reading them, you are not reading somebody else's letters, nor are you reading pieces of history. These letters are written for *you*! Unless you realise this, you will not be spiritually nourished by the light, wisdom and love that are here directed especially at you.

In our chosen study, the Holy Spirit is telling us that we are in no way defenceless in our stand against evil: God has amply provided for our protection in this fallen world. We are told to stand. We don't have to advance and take territory: we stand victorious in Jesus Christ. Satan wants to topple us from this happy position; he wants us back. The analogy throughout is that of armour, and the example given is that of the Roman soldiers who were prevalent at the time this letter was written.

SECTION 10

Our stand against evil is an important aspect of our faith. William Gurnall obviously thought so: he wrote a three-volume tome on the subject, entitled, *The Christian in Complete Armour*. Anybody who has read this amazing work cannot help but be inspired. This section is built around notes that I took while reading this excellent work.

Prayer: *Heavenly Father, may the words that I am about to study fill me with confidence in the protection that You afford me. May I be a credit to You, and remain faithful in my conflict with evil, for Your Word reminds me that I stand victorious in Jesus Christ. I ask this in Jesus' precious name. Amen.*

Verse 10 is a call to arms, a call for courage. It's a call to service, and a reminder that we need strength in the Lord: *"... apart from Me you can do nothing"* (John 15: 5). The Christian must be armed (v 11). Jesus is our complete armour; we must *"clothe ourselves with the Lord Jesus Christ"* (Rom 13: 14).

The Christian's armour has been especially designed by God, and each part has its special function. Each piece is perfect, and God will train us to use it properly. The armour must be put on, and it must be kept on. Why do we need any armour? Satan is the short answer. Satan is a tempter, an accuser, a liar and a seducer. He wants us back into his kingdom. What else do we know about Satan, whom Scripture calls *"the prince of the world"*? Well, his will is termed the *"law of sin"* (Rom 8: 2). He not only claims his throne by conquest, he also claims it by election. Jesus said to Satan's followers, *"You belong to your father, the devil, and you want to carry out your father's desire"*. Satan will also try to counterfeit God's spiritual gifts; we must indeed "test the spirits".

Satan's power is depicted in Scripture as *"a roaring lion"*

Example Bible Study 5

and *"a strong man"*. Satan is *"the god of this world"*. His aim is for the souls of man; our bodies are only secondary. However, God will not permit Satan to infiltrate our souls. Satan needs our permission to do that, or he needs to find our souls vacant or abandoned. This is why fringe meditation practices are so dangerous. We must never vacate or blank out our minds or wills.

Satan attacks the borders of our faith; his kingdom is the darkness of the world. So what are his tricks? Well, the most popular one is to make us think that he does not even exist. When that fails, he will try to keep Christians too busy to have times for God. He tries to intercept thoughts of God's grace, mercy and peace. He also tries to interfere with a sinner's true repentance. He will try to suggest a compromise, such as a very mild confession. He will try to ensure that sinners do not go very far from their sins. Scripture has also shown Satan interfering with God's messages. Perhaps his major trick is to make Christians doubt their place in Jesus. He will highlight our faults, while also highlighting God's hatred of sin. He will do all he can to promote a 'salvation by works' campaign.

So we must wrestle (v 12), enlisting God as a second. We should be careful to ensure that we are not wrestling against God's Spirit or against God's providence; we cannot attribute everything we dislike as the work of Satan. Neither do we wrestle in our own strength.

Verse 13 gives a second, repeated exhortation. This is because of our need for perseverance and of our need to examine ourselves. Days of evil will come, Jesus has assured us of this. We are to stand; we do not need to move. We should also remember the fact that there is no covering at the back of our armour: we do not turn our backs on Satan. We must stand our own ground. God has assigned to us our own special place; He does not hold us accountable for another person's watch. We

SECTION 10

simply cannot shoulder burdens that God has not told us to carry. We are to be watchful at all times and not fall asleep or be half-hearted in our fight against evil.

Now we come to the **armour** itself. Putting on the armour is something we must do. God does not put it on for us. It should be worn in anticipation of days of evil, not hastily assembled while under attack.

The first piece described is the **belt of truth** (v 14). This not only refers to truth of doctrine; it also refers to sincerity. The belt that is the truth of doctrine is a girdle for the mind: a foundation of spiritual truth. We should beware of curiosity about other faiths. We should meditate on God's Word and walk in the power of His Holy Spirit.

The belt of truth is also for truth of heart: a girdle for the will. This is truthfulness, or sincerity. Hypocrisy intrudes on worship and promotes self: only green leaves are shown, instead of flowers or fruit. A hypocrite keeps God's gifts for himself, instead of displaying the attractive flower that is Jesus Christ or fruit that others can receive. Sincerity covers the joints of our armour, whereas hypocrisy leaves gaps. Sincerity makes the heart willing and open to God. If any hypocrisy is found in us, we must face up to the fact and take it to Jesus. We cannot cure our own hypocrisy. Sincerity is the first piece of armour mentioned and the last piece to be put on. It holds firm our breastplate and displays our true colours: those of Jesus Christ, and not ourselves or Satan.

Next, we come to the breastplate itself (v 14): The **breastplate of righteousness**. This is holiness. The breastplate covers the heart, and makes us bold. Holiness makes a good foundation and protects us against guilt. It motivates purity, by using Jesus

Example Bible Study 5

as an example. It depends on God and seeks out other spiritual companions. It helps guard against discouragement and holds no fear whatsoever of death and condemnation. Satan will say that righteousness hinders pleasure, wastes prosperity and invites worldly opposition – tell him to get lost!

The **spiritual footwear,** described in verse 15, protects our steps, making travel easier. The readiness of the Gospel of peace: The Gospel is good news, and our spiritual armour enables this news to travel speedily and safely. Peace here means reconciliation with God, bringing with it peace of conscience. It also helps us to cope with suffering. "Readiness" – for what? We must be ready for trials, and be willing to deny 'self'. We must be ready to accept God's will as being in our best interests. This special footwear lifts us above danger.

The **shield of faith** (v 16) to extinguish the flaming arrows: faith helps us receive strength from Jesus; it defends all of our other Christian attributes. The Holy Spirit promotes faith by illuminating our understanding, convicting our consciences and by renewal. This enables us to elect Jesus as our Saviour, which in turn fosters obedience, prayer and expectancy. We can protect our faith by reading the Word of God and by looking into our consciences and dealing with unbelief. We must believe our beliefs and doubt our doubts! What are the flaming arrows? Well, temptation is perhaps the most common one, followed by doubt, despair and distorting God's true, loving nature.

The **helmet of salvation** (v 17) is hope. Christian hope is different from worldly hope. Worldly hope usually involves wishful thinking: "it may or may not happen, but I hope it will". The Christian hope is absolute certainty. The helmet defends

SECTION 10

the mind and makes the heart bold. Hope sees worldly pleasures for what they are. It calms us under affliction and fills us with joy. Hope enables the soul to wait; God's timing is always perfect. We can help to preserve hope by studying the Word, keeping a pure conscience, prayer and recalling God's past mercies.

The **sword of the Spirit** (v 17) is the Word of God – for attack and defence. Christians are ineffective without God's Word. The Holy Spirit, the sword, is the author and interpreter of Scripture. He gives the Word its power. This whole study is about the "Sword of the Spirit".

Finally, **pray in the Spirit on all occasions** (v 18). We are to be alert; we are to be watchful. We must add prayer to our armour at all times.

An amusing parlour game could be invented. A prize could be given to the person who can think of the most phrases that Satan uses. What would be his most-used phrase? I would put forward two: "Isn't that annoying" and "I wouldn't stand for that!" For example, in order to promote disharmony, Satan could convince a wife that a habit of her husband, one that she had previously found quite endearing, is actually getting on her nerves: "Isn't that annoying?" The wife would then point out this 'annoying' habit to her husband, suggesting that he should try to stop it. In steps Satan again, this time to the husband: "I wouldn't let her speak to me like that! Who does she think she is?" Before long, we have a blazing row on our hands, simply because of Satan's input!

Yes, we must be watchful and never lower our guard. As William Gurnall says: Our armour, like our bodies, is not to be taken off until we don our white robes in heaven!

"But these things are written so that
you might believe that Jesus is the Christ,
the Son of God, and by believing
you may have life in His name."
(John 20: 31)

"... test the spirits to see whether
they are from God,
because many false prophets
have gone out into the world."
(1 John 4: 1).

Section Eleven

What Contradictions?

So how can we believe the Bible to be any kind of guide, when in one part, it seems to tell you one thing; in another, it tells you something else? This is the way many ask who have only a fleeting acquaintance with the Word of God. Nevertheless, if the Bible were the reliable Word of God that I claim it to be, then even one proven contradiction would seriously undermine any claim that I make in respect of its reliability. I can honestly say that I know of no supposed contradiction that has not been satisfactorily explained. If only we would read our Bibles prayerfully, invoking the presence of the Holy Spirit, then we would see these so-called contradictions disappear.

In this section we shall look at some areas where difficulties may arise. I was originally going to limit this to instances where the Bible may seem to disagree with itself. I was not going to address creation disputes with scientists and historians. However, it does seem that many people will not accept the Bible as any kind of authority while it appears to them to be in error over what it tells us about the beginning of the world. Or is John Blanchard nearer the truth when he says, "Men do not reject the Bible because they find fault in it, but because it finds fault in them." Francis Schaeffer insists, "The

What Contradictions?

ordinary Christian with the Bible in his hand can say that the majority is wrong."

Of course, there are also the views of other Christians to be considered. Many of them will suggest that my treatment of the age of the earth in my first book was a cop-out, an appeasement to science. Well, in a sense they are right. You see, I expected most readers to assume that the earth is millions of years old – after all, both this and evolution are taught in our schools as fact. Rather than alienate my readers within such a limited space and so early in my book, I expounded the 'gap theory' in the hope that we could then move on to matters that are far more important.

Up until now, I have always limited myself to glib statements, such as, "How can nothing explode!" in response to the Big Bang theorists. I would ask Darwin's advocates, "Where are the fossils of the intermediate stages of evolution!" I had never undertaken a thorough, prayerful study of this subject – I never felt the need. Well, I now have, and I am somewhat surprised by the results! However, before I begin on this, I want to point out that there are some 1,189 chapters in the Bible. The Holy Spirit has only devoted 2 of these chapters to the account of the creation. The measure of importance we place on any subject in Scripture should, I feel, reflect the number of chapters allocated to that subject – and yet, so many Christians seem to be obsessed with creation theories!

So what exactly does God tell us about the beginnings? I place the following in what I take to be chronological order:

"In the beginning ..." (Gen 1: 1 / John 1: 1)
"... was the Word [Jesus], *and the Word was with God, and the Word was God. He was with God in the beginning."*
(John 1: 1-2)
"... God created the heavens and the earth." (Gen 1: 1)
"Through Him [Jesus] *all things were made; without Him*

SECTION 11

nothing was made that has been made." (John 1: 3) The heavens and the earth were made – completely.

"Now the earth [not the stars or the heavens] *became formless and empty, darkness was over the surface of the deep ..."* (Gen 1: 2).

Whatever had previously happened, the world was now in darkness and apparently flooded. Now God could create His masterpiece – you and me! (Eph 2: 10)

"... And the [Holy] *Spirit of God was hovering over the waters."* (Gen 1: 2) The earth was flooded; but this was not Noah's flood. It was as if the earth had undergone a kind of baptism. Now, the Holy Sprit could be brought into action.

"And God said, 'Let there be light', and there was light" (Gen 1: 2).

"In Him [Jesus] *was life and that life was the light of men. The light shines in the darkness, but the darkness has not overpowered it."* (John 1: 4-5) How appropriate that following the earth's 'baptism' and the movement of the Holy Spirit, we are now shown the Light of the world, Jesus Christ! Jesus is the Alpha and the Omega, the beginning and the end.

"[Jesus said] *I am the Light of the world."* (John 9: 5) Just as at the end of all things the sun and moon will not give out their light, so here at this new beginning, the Light of Jesus is sufficient for all things.

"God saw that the light was good, and He separated the light from the darkness. God called the light 'day', and the darkness he called 'night' ... the first day" (Gen 1: 4-5).

"And God said, 'Let there be ... sky [or, let the sky again become visible from earth] *... the second day."* (Gen 1: 6-8) God had lifted the clouds from earth, exposing the sky – a sky of clouds.

"The Lord reigns, let the earth be glad;
let the distant shores rejoice.
Clouds and thick darkness surround Him;

What Contradictions?

Righteousness and justice are the foundations of His throne."
(Psalm 97: 1-2)
At first, our knowledge of God is unclear and soulish. We need a spiritual rebirth in order to penetrate that 'cloud of unknowing'.
"And God said, 'Let the water be gathered to one place [following the flood] *and let dry land appear' "*... 'land' and ... 'seas' ... Then *"God said, 'Let the land produce vegetation, seed-bearing crops and trees that bear fruit with seed in it, according to their various kinds' ... the third day."* (Gen 1: 9-13)
"And God said, 'Let there be lights in the expanse of the sky to separate day from night, and let them serve as signs to mark seasons and days and years' ... the fourth day." (Gen 1: 14-19)
The word used in these first days means 'make to appear' rather than 'create'. The clouds have gone. Lights that were always there would again be visible and act as signs. God wanted to be sought after and known by His creation. The man He was to create was to interpret the seasons and be able to 'number his days'; his sights are to be heavenward.

Despite any reservations that scientists and meteorologists might have with the above account, I can believe that God could deliver the above in four twenty-four-hour days. For the account of the next two days, we shall require all of our faith. However, we are talking about Almighty God! Before we look at day 5 and day 6, let's remember that Jesus commanded a storm to be instantly calm. He walked on the water. Jesus instantly provided fish enough to feed five thousand people. He brought back to life a person who had been dead for days. There were eyewitnesses to each of these events – in some cases, thousands. Jesus said that God could raise children of Abraham from nearby stones. He said that if we have even small faith, we could command a mountain to move, and it

SECTION 11

would move – instantly!
"For He [God] *spoke, and it came to be."* (Psalm 33: 9)

Let us therefore now take what little faith we have into the next days of the creation account:

"And God said, 'Let the waters teem with living creatures, and let birds fly above the expanse of the sky ... according to their kinds' ... the fifth day." (Gen 1: 20-23)
"And God said, 'Let the land produce living creatures according to their kinds' " ... The dinosaurs have gone! Whatever might have happened before, God is here creating everything 'according to their kinds'. This seems to me to rule out the evolution of today's birds and animals. In the next 'day', we shall see that 'making man in our likeness' seems to rule out evolution for us.

Now we see the crowning moment of God's new work!
"Then God said, 'Let us [Father, Son and Holy Spirit] *make man in our image, in our likeness* [a trinity: body, soul and spirit], *and let them rule over ... all of the creatures that move along the ground' ... male and female He created them ... God blessed them and said to them, 'Be fruitful and increase in number; fill the earth and subdue it ... rule over every living creature that moves on the ground' "* (Gen 1: 26-28) Here they are: the new man and woman – a new creation! Just as we have to be born anew into the kingdom of God, so here we see man being created anew, in God's likeness.

On the other hand, however, there are many Christians who interpret the biblical use of 'day' to mean 'period of time' and they refer to the verse *"With the Lord a day is like a thousand years, and a thousand years are like a day"* (2 Peter 3: 8) to support this view. They also believe that the creation of the

What Contradictions?

living creatures was a gradual, evolutionary process, but guided and directed by God until the time came when He breathed His Spirit into homo sapiens.

Something often overlooked comes next:

"Then God said, 'I give you every seed-bearing plant ... they will be yours for food [It is only after the 'Fall' and Noah's flood (see below) that God told man to eat meat, which was indicative of our need of a Saviour] ... *And to all the beasts of the earth and all the birds of the air ... I give every green plant for food'* [Carnivores and birds of prey only ate meat after the earth was fallen; before that – and, as God intended – they only ate green plants!] ... *And God saw all that He had made, and it was very good ... the sixth day"* (Gen 1: 29-31).

The Bible then tells us that God 'rested' on the seventh day, and inaugurated this Sabbath rest for each of His children.

God wanted His children to properly commune with Him. Therefore, when the time was right, He established His 'Nation of priests'. A priest is a mediator between God and His people. The Israelites, this nation of priests, were meant to teach the whole world how to know, love and worship its Creator. This nation would begin with one specially created man.

Yes, I am suggesting that the creation of God's chosen people was probably later than the creation described in Chapter 1 of Genesis. This seems to be especially true for those who consider the 'days' described in Chapter 1 to be long periods of time rather than twenty-four hour days. In this case, to claim that the account of the Garden of Eden is merely an amplification of day six in Chapter 1 is at odds with God declaring everything 'very good' at the completion of that sixth 'day'. No, if the sixth day was a significant number of years, then things were certainly not 'very good' in God's eyes at the end of that period of time. Similarly, God would not have said that the animals and mankind were to eat herbs after man's Fall,

SECTION 11

if the Fall occurred within the period of time covered by that 'day'.

But I feel that we are meant to consider the creation account in Chapter 1 as periods of twenty-four hours, and I have described it as such above. This is emphasised by the phrase 'evening and morning' at the end of each day. If we are talking about twenty-four hour periods – then, yes, the sixth day might include Adam's creation, in which case the Fall would have occurred after that twenty-four hour creation period – and all was indeed 'very good' before the Fall.

However, I do now tend to think that the creation in the garden occurred later. If this is the case, then first, the Lord had to create the garden.

God was to create a special nation in a special place – a garden, an earthly paradise. He did this in a barren area, one not previously inhabited by man. Many times, translators of the Bible have used the word 'earth' when 'land' would be more appropriate. We get this in the story of Noah's flood, where 'the waters covered the earth' is used instead of 'the waters covered the land'. If you read the story of Noah, replacing the word 'earth' with the word 'land', you will see that the flood was probably local, mainly involving God's specially chosen people, people who had consistently disobeyed Him. They and their land also had to go through a form of 'baptism'. It was after this (local) flood that God told mankind to eat meat. At the site of the proposed Garden of Eden, no rain had appeared in this barren land.

"For the Lord God had not sent rain on the earth [this land], *and there was no man* [in the area] *to work the ground, but streams came up and watered the whole surface of the ground – the Lord formed man from the dust of the ground and breathed into his nostrils the breath of life, and the man became a living being."* (Gen 2: 4-7)

What Contradictions?

I don't have to retell the story of Adam and Eve here; we are all familiar with it. But I should point out that many Christians regard this story (Gen 2: 4b-3: 24) as an allegory. They cannot accept that the tree of knowledge of good and evil could be anything but allegorical. They believe that this parable was given by God to express the moral failure of mankind to maintain a good relationship with their Creator. They rejected His fatherly guidance in favour of "I'll do it MY WAY!"

Angels (spiritual, heavenly creatures) had been in existence since the very beginning:
"Where were you when I laid the earth's foundation? Tell me, if you understand. Who marked off its dimensions? Surely you know! Who stretched a measuring line across it? On what were its footings set, or who laid its cornerstone – while the morning stars sang together, and all the angels shouted for joy?" (Job 38: 4-7)

However, one angel rebelled against God: *"How you have fallen from heaven, O morning star, son of the dawn! You have been cast down to the earth, you who once laid low the nations! You said in your heart, I will ascend to heaven; I will raise my throne above the stars of God; I will sit enthroned on the mount of the assembly, on the utmost heights of the sacred mountain. I will ascend above the tops of the clouds; I will make myself like the Most High"* (Isaiah 14: 12-14).

Yes, Lucifer, the 'Morning Star' or Satan, as we best know him, will soon be making an appearance! God was creating His special people and Satan wanted to thwart God's plans. Satan seduced Eve, and she and Adam ate the forbidden fruit.

God gave the earth over to the kingship of Satan, for nothing sinful may stand before God. As a result, all of mankind has chosen to decide for itself what is right and wrong. Rather than obey God, mankind preferred to be led by the

SECTION 11

corrupt world, the lustful flesh and the devil – whom the Word of God calls the 'ruler of this world'.

"[Jesus said] This is the verdict [or this is the judgement]: Light has come into the world but men loved darkness instead of Light because their deeds were evil." (John 3: 19)

Of course, by placing the creation of humans before Adam and Eve we provide Cain with a wife. Without this, we would have to accommodate incest into our reasoning. It also accounts for the many different races on earth, all of which were created by God in Genesis 1. Making the story of Adam and Eve to be a special and separate creation is significant in many other ways. I expected to have to twist many verses of Scripture to accommodate it, but it was not the case. Indeed, many slightly difficult passages become instantly clearer. We can now better understand what Paul meant by his image of the Potter using some of His clay for special purposes, while the rest were not (Rom 9: 20-24). We can better appreciate Jesus saying that He had come initially for the Jews, God's specially created people. We can better picture the fact that we as Gentiles are 'grafted in' to the true tree (Rom 11: 17), and that we are indeed God's adopted children (Ephesians 1: 5).

The only verse I had some initial problems with was:
"From one man he made every nation of men, that they should inhabit the whole earth; and He determined the times set for them and the exact places where they should live." (Acts 17: 26). 'From one man' is better translated 'From one blood', or 'From one source'. This passage in Acts concludes with, *"We are His* [God's] *offspring."* (vv 28,29)

Yes, Exodus 20: 11 tells us that in six days God created the heavens and the earth, but here the emphasis is on comparing God's creation days with our calendar week. God was inaugurating the weekly Sabbath rest for His children. Again, 'created' could be read 'made to appear'.

What Contradictions?

But, what about death – Romans 5: 12 says, *"Therefore, just as sin entered the world through one man [Adam], and death through sin, and in this way death came to all men, because all sinned ..."* Some suggest that there could not have been life before Adam, because they claim that this verse says that physical death began with Adam. But is it really saying that? This passage goes on to say, *"For before the Law was given, sin was in the world. But sin is not taken into account when there is no law. Nevertheless, death reigned from the time of Adam to the time of Moses, even over those who did not sin by breaking a command, as did Adam, who was a pattern of the One to come."* God had intended that His specially chosen people should not see death; they were to inaugurate a spiritual kingdom. We see glimpses of this in the lives of Enoch and Elijah, but this plan was thwarted at the start when Adam sinned. Because of that sin, physical death also came to the Israelites. Thereafter, death now indeed came to all people (including the Israelites). Jesus was to put all that right. Paul goes on to say that our Lord's redemptive act was far greater than Adam's sin, because, thanks to Jesus, atonement is available to all people, and not just Adam's descendants.

Doesn't this mean that all Gentiles are free from the blame for Adam's sin, if they are not descended from him? No, because the Word says that there is no one righteous, not even one (Rom 3: 10). Where there is no Law, there is no imputed sin. As adopted children we are grafted into God's family, including its inheritance. When the Holy Spirit approaches us, one of His first jobs is to convict us of our sin. He places us in the light of God's Word, and in the light of that Word we stand guilty. When we are confronted with the righteous Law, we are stricken by it, and we are immediately in need of a Saviour. Thanks to Jesus, that salvation is now available to all.

But do I actually believe all this? Do I really believe in my heart that Adam and Eve were a special creation, and not the

SECTION 11

first humans? Well, it goes against everything that I have accepted since I was a child, but it does seem to make sense.

Although some say that we are to treat the Adam and Eve section of Genesis as a parable or an allegory, it does seem to me that the whole of Genesis, including the account of the Garden of Eden, was written in such a way as to be believed as literal fact. For those like me who believe the Bible to be the literal Word of God, it seems that the only alternative to something like the above would be to stand with our faithful brothers and sisters who consider the earth to be no more than ten thousand years old, and I have to admit to finding that difficult.

This study on the creation was inserted here after the trilogy had been completed, and after Book 1 was published. My books are aimed at those who have received something of a 'spark' from God; they are not evangelistic or 'cold-calling' works. I could therefore say in Book 1 that, spiritually, God sees only two persons, Adam or Jesus. We who have received a calling from God are either associated with fallen man, Adam, or we are in a relationship with Jesus. Those who have never been confronted with the Word of God are indeed on the outside. They will be judged on the basis of Romans 1: 20 - *"For since the creation of the world God's invisible qualities – His eternal power and divine nature – have been clearly seen, so that men are without excuse."* – and Romans 2: 14-15 – *"Indeed, when the Gentiles, who do not have the Law, do by nature things required of the Law, they are a law for themselves, even though they do not have the Law, since they show that the requirements of the Law are written on their hearts, their consciences also bearing witness, and their thoughts now accusing, now even defending them."*

What Contradictions?

I believe C S Lewis perfectly summed up those verses from Romans in his book 'Mere Christianity'. In this book he explains that we all – in this society, and in every society there has ever been – have evidence of a 'moral code' of right and wrong in our hearts, a moral code that proves the existence of a creator, the author of a basic moral code. Whether people are 'religious' or not, they have a sense in themselves of what is basically right and what is wrong – it is impressed on their consciences.

Some people insist that all of the various religions are really praying to the same God. They claim that these are simply different routes to the same place. As I have just said, most of the fundamental truths are embedded in the hearts of most societies – do not murder, steal, lie or commit adultery – God has in most cases made sure of that, even though some – a minority – have twisted His laws out of recognition. Apart from these basics, which are apparent in all of the various religions, they do not all say the same thing and they do not all teach the same truths. If someone was to approach my friends, saying: "That Dave Bull: he visits brothels; he is a drug dealer and he is a staunch supporter of Apartheid," I trust that my friends would say to that person that he is not describing the Dave Bull that they know – I trust that they would insist that I am being confused with somebody else. Well, that is exactly how I feel when other religions describe their God; they are certainly not describing the God of the Bible that I know and love. They are certainly not praying to the Father that Jesus revealed to us – and they are certainly not teaching what Jesus taught. Nevertheless, those that are brought up on the Word of God will be subject to the judgement of the Law – unless they are in Jesus, in which case the judgement of their sins has already taken place at Calvary.

SECTION 11

Before moving on, let me first try to dispel any false notions some may have of hell and eternal punishment. How anyone who knows and loves the Lord can possibly think that He would condemn people who are ignorant of Him to an eternity of torture beggars belief! Hell is a place designed and designated for Satan – and for all who choose to follow him. For others found guilty in the Judgement there is no eternal torture; there is annihilation. The 'grinding of teeth' is describing those who, after they have died, realise that the Word of God is true and that they must now face the One they have rejected or mocked. It is rather like the picture given to us in the story of Lazarus and Dives (Luke 16: 19-31). Yes, no one comes to Almighty God except through Jesus at the Judgement of all souls. Those convicted at the Judgement will be instantly annihilated – the 'second death'; in other words, complete, eternal and final death. Their (dead) bodies will be *"thrown into the lake of fire"*. The verse, *"Where their worm does not die, and the fire is not quenched"* (Mark 9: 48) simply tells us that there will be no resurrection from this second death.

The sins of Christians have already faced judgement at Calvary; our judgement will result in rewards or lack of rewards. It is God's design that the Gospels be preached throughout the world – that everybody will hear the Word of God and believe in His Son, for all who do will inherit eternal life. It is our commission to spread this Word and help procure for all eternity the lives of those that Jesus died to save.

Let us now rejoin this Section. Let's now consider how some parts of God's Word might be seen to be contradictory:

One area of concern is where the Gospel writers seem to differ. In these cases, they are all correct! They are usually giving descriptions of different parts of the same story. The first Bible 'contradiction' that I ever noticed was in the old King James Version. In this, John tells us that Barabbas was a

What Contradictions?

robber, whereas Mark reports him as being a murderer. Of course, he was both. A highwayman who happened to have killed a man will be known in the town of the victim as a murderer; generally, he will be known as a robber.

It is certain that the later Gospel writers knew what the earlier ones had written. As each Gospel has its own particular slant, they would each include some details that the others would have considered less important. I have already mentioned elsewhere that John's Gospel is different from the other 'synoptic' Gospels. We need not be concerned if the sequence of events is different from the others in John's hands. John is mainly concerned with the spiritual significance of events; he is not concerned with their chronological order.

Perhaps the most commonly cited instance of contradiction is the one where people compare "an eye for an eye" with "turn the other cheek". In the former instance, God was addressing the perpetrators of violence, saying that He will require retribution from them equal to the crime. On the other hand, Jesus said, "turn the other cheek" to the potential victims of crime. Jesus is saying that it is not for us to seek revenge; God shall avenge us. Both passages are therefore stating the same truth: "Revenge is mine, says the Lord".

Some cite instances where God promised actions He would take, but that were not subsequently carried out. Such a case is that reported in Jonah, regarding the town of Nineveh. Most of God's judgements are conditional on man's response. In God's eyes, if that man (or nation) changes, then they are not the same people that He had previously addressed.

It should be said that Bible scholars take the Bible to be the Word of God as it was originally written. I am given to believe that the difference in the symbols for many biblical numbers is very small. Apparently, a slight accent or stroke can add thousands to a number. Even in our writing, a single dot can change £10000 to £100.00. As the original manuscripts are

SECTION 11

preserved only in copies, one would expect human error. However, surely we can believe that God is not only able to create His Word through the hearts of His Spirit-filled children; He is also able to preserve it intact.

Sarcasm and irony are both common in Scripture; of course, instances of these should not be taken literally. We should also not take other figures of speech literally.

Jesus came to earth having emptied Himself of His former glory, and by consent, became 'inferior' to His Father. In His pre-incarnate state and now, in His risen glory, He was and is equal to God. Passages referring to Jesus may seem to contradict when talking about different times. Similarly, we should remember that God talks differently about believing Christians than He does non-believers. We should not confuse God's words to one group with those addressed to the other.

Names of places, mountains, rivers and people were all likely to change. Indeed, for all these things there was often more than one name. Different names were often used according to the nationality of the person or the place in which an incident is described, in Babylonia, for example.

It has to be said that women were often omitted from reports of Old Testament events and from statistics. We should now appreciate just what a huge influence Christianity has been on the role of woman in the world.

People's different interpretations of what the Bible is telling us do not count as contradiction. There have been discussions on the difference between the judgement of nations and the judgement of individuals. Some insist that there is a difference between 'entering the Kingdom of Heaven' and 'being saved and inheriting eternal life'. These issues are both outside the scope of this section.

Another point that I am not going to expand here is the fact that something that seems to be a contradiction in normal terms need not be a spiritual contradiction. As I have said before,

What Contradictions?

spiritual things are not bound by the restrictions of time and space.

Some people find John's first letter confusing. At a first glance, it may seem that perfection is expected. Verse 6 of Chapter 3 says, *"No one who lives in Him keeps on sinning. No one who continues to sin has either seen Him or known Him."* While verse 9 of the same chapter says, *"No one who is born of God will continue to sin, because God's seed remains in him; he cannot go on sinning because he has been born of God."* However, this same letter had already said, *"If we claim to be without sin, we deceive ourselves and the truth is not in us. If we confess our sins, He is faithful and just and will forgive our sins and purify us from all unrighteousness"* (Chapter 1: 8-9). John is here concerned with deliberate and repeated sinning. However, it was not until I heard a lovely story about a motorist that I could finally taste the full flavour of John's letter:

The story is of a man who loved motoring; he always dreamed that one day he would own a Rolls Royce. Well, at last he bought one. He loved his car, and the car responded to the care and affection he gave to it. After a year or two, he took the car on a driving holiday through Europe. It broke down in France! He telephoned Rolls Royce, and they promised to take care of the problem. Sure enough: in no time, a mechanic arrived and the car was fixed. When our motorist returned to England, he winced at the thought of how much the repair would cost him, especially as the mechanic had to be sent to France. A few weeks went by – no bill. Being an honest man, when a further few weeks had passed, he telephoned Rolls Royce to explain about the breakdown and to say that he had not received a bill. The man at Rolls Royce said, "With respect sir, I fear you must be mistaken: Rolls Royce cars do not break down." Of course, the car did break down, but in the maker's eyes, it did not – such a thing is unthinkable; and there was no price to pay for the repair! However, looking at it in this way

SECTION 11

should not lead us to think we have a "licence to sin", but rather that because we have a "Rolls Royce Saviour", we are going to be kept by Him from sinning.

Some say that a contradiction appears in Proverbs Chapter 26, when one compares verses 4 and 5. You may be interested to look this up now. Although giving different advice in the same situation, verse 4 teaches us that if we act in the way that a fool does, then we become fools ourselves. Verse 5 says that if we respond to a fool in the same way that we respond to a wise man, the fool will think he also is wise.

I believe I have now touched on the main areas that are most likely to be considered contradictions. It is easy to forget that we Christians receive regular revelation from God. We must therefore be patient with those who do not have this regular enlightenment. We must not forget that there once was a time when the Word of God was not as clear to us as it now is.

Bearing in mind what has been discussed in this section, let us now return to that glorious Sunday, that first Easter morning. From all four Gospel accounts, we can now see how the complete sequence of these wonderful events unfolded:

In order to embalm the Lord's body, the two Marys, Joanna, Salome and other women went with spices to the tomb. When they arrived, they noticed that the stone was no longer in place. Not only had there been an earthquake, an angel had rolled away the stone and sat on it. The guards, who had been ordered to watch over the sepulchre, became "like dead men" through terror. Not aware that Jesus had risen, the women entered the tomb to find that the body was missing. They were puzzled. Mary Magdalene, thinking that the body had been stolen, left the other women and ran to tell Peter and John. The others remained in the tomb. Two angels then appeared. They confirmed the fact that Jesus had risen and gave the women

What Contradictions?

words for the apostles. These women then left to find the disciples.

Meanwhile, Peter and John, who were staying at a different place from the other disciples, heard what Mary Magdalene had to say. They ran ahead of her to the sepulchre. They found it empty, with the grave clothes and napkin left tidily folded. This convinced John that the body had not been forcibly removed or taken by friends. He started to believe that his Lord had risen. The two then returned to the city. Mary Magdalene, who had followed Peter and John, but had not caught up with them, stood weeping alone outside the sepulchre. She saw two angels. Turning around, she saw Jesus. He gave her comfort, and asked her to pass on His assurances to the disciples. On their way back, the other women also saw Jesus. He endorsed the word that the angels had given them. True to life, some of the people involved concentrated on different aspects of what happened, including the number of angels – it probably wasn't important to them how many, in view of the almost unbelievable fact that Jesus had been restored to life!

Matthew beautifully wraps everything up with the Great Commission from the Lord: "All authority in heaven and on earth has been given to Me. Therefore go and make disciples of all nations, baptising them in the name of the Father and of the Son and of the Holy Spirit, and teaching them to obey everything I have commanded you. And surely I am with you always, to the very end of the age" (Matt 28; 18-20).

Wonderful!

"For certain men whose condemnation
was written about long ago
have secretly slipped in among you.
They are godless men, who change
the grace of our God
into a licence for immorality and deny
Jesus Christ our only Sovereign and Lord"
(Jude v 4)

"If Christ has not been raised,
our preaching is useless and so is our faith ...
And if Christ has not been raised,
your faith is futile; you are still in your sins."
(1 Cor 15: 14 & 17)

Section Twelve

The Liberal Church

This series cannot claim to be a scholarly work. In my determination to keep these books short, I have seldom taken space to explain any opposing views while making a point on any subject. Well, this promises to be an extremely opinionated section, one that should be read critically and prayerfully!

I have learnt over the years that Jesus calls us to lead a life of simplicity in this complicated, hectic world; He calls us to show love, peace and mercy to all we meet. This I have tried to do, despite my natural tendency to be overly shy, somewhat restless and with a fondness for cleverness. Jesus showed everybody the love, peace and mercy of His Father. Only the arrogant felt the weight of Jesus' wrath. Whenever those in positions of authority misrepresented the Word of God Jesus showed His righteous indignation. Whilst I have tried to be simple, helpful and positive in this series, I too feel the need to speak negatively about some of the things that go on in our churches today.

It seems to me that whenever the Church gets a mention in the national press, it is all too often in respect of its members' lack of belief or because of its members' sexual antics. We have all read about bishops, those who proudly announce that

The Liberal Church

they don't believe in the resurrection of our Lord. We have also read of homosexual church members who claim for themselves all sorts of outrageous demands. Add to this the public dispute over the ordination of women, and we have a corporation not exactly increasing its appeal to would-be members.

Of course, I'm mainly talking about the Anglican Church, the Church of England. Happily, most other denominations would not tolerate such things. What has happened in the Church of England? I know it used to be the done thing to go to Church. Anyone in business used to get brownie points for being an honest church-going person; non-worshippers used to be frowned upon. Surely, all that has now changed. Surely, all we should now have left are true believers – the remnant: committed people that God can use as building blocks for His kingdom – those who attend for no other reason than to worship God in fellowship or those making honest enquiries?

It would appear that the same could not be said of the leadership of the Church, as some of its bishops are seen to display an open disregard for the Word of God. Of course, I am not talking about all bishops. The Church has many that are a real blessing to the Lord. I just hope that I'm talking about a minority! However, on television current affairs programmes, with their potential congregation of millions, I have seldom heard a bishop even mention the name of Jesus; whereas the ordinary preachers do.

One has only to sample the Bible's teaching letters. In these, the Holy Spirit seldom goes more than a few verses without mentioning Jesus by name. I was sitting watching television with my wife Maureen, when we noticed that the Archbishop of Canterbury was about to deliver his message to bring in the New Year. I suggested that we should count how many times he mentions the Lord Jesus in his bid to welcome in 2004. Not once! Not once did the leader of Christ's people deem it important or appropriate enough to mention Jesus'

SECTION 12

Name.

Surely it is essential for every employee of the Church to believe in the death and resurrection of Jesus Christ. As our introductory text reminds us: our faith is futile if Jesus is not risen; and, more seriously, we are still in our sins. What on earth draws non-believers into the Church? Would not a position in politics or the social services be a better vocation for humanists? Each would-be bishop has to "affirm, and accordingly declare [his] belief in the faith which is revealed in the Holy Scriptures and set forth in the catholic creeds". Am I putting it too strongly if I suggest that those who take up positions in our churches deceive people, accept money under false pretences and betray vows taken before God, if they do not believe in the resurrection of Jesus Christ?

The fact that we are part of an Established Church is one reason for our problems. It might not seem like it, but England is officially still a Christian country: so far, so good. Unfortunately, politicians promote clergy into the highest positions. How can we trust unbelieving politicians to select and promote the most spiritual shepherds of the flock of England? Consequently, we have many instances where Spirit-filled Christian ministers are receiving their guidance from non-believing humanist bishops!

Prayer: *Almighty and everlasting God, who alone work great marvels, send down upon our bishops and curates, and all congregations committed to their charge, the healthful Spirit of Your grace; and so that they may truly please You, pour out upon them the continual dew of Your blessing. Grant this, O Lord, for the honour of our Advocate and Mediator, Jesus Christ. Amen.*

(Adapted from the Book of Common Prayer)

The Liberal Church

This brings me uneasily to the case of practising homosexuals within the Church. God calls their acts *"detestable"* in the Old Testament (Lev 18: 22), when it was punishable by death, and in the New Testament *"degrading their bodies with one another"* (Rom 1: 24) where forgiveness may be obtained. And yet many bishops have knowingly employed practising homosexuals as ministers! God loves each homosexual, but He hates the sin they commit. Jesus died for every one of them. Can homosexuals be saved? Of course, if their faith and trust is in Jesus, but if they cannot remain celibate they will probably remain babies in Christ – and they should certainly never become leaders! Those who are able to live celibate lives can be excellent, Spirit-filled leaders. If I am right about what I said in the last section, then those who commit homosexual acts will know deep within them that what they are doing is wrong and at variance with God's Word. As we saw in Psalm 32, God will wait until they confess their sins; only then can He really help them. Homosexual practice is not a special sin: it is just that its advocates are being blinded to the fact that it is a sin; this is what makes it a special case.

No, we are not bound by the Law, but if God's Word calls something we are doing "detestable", then we must surely do something about it; we must take it to Jesus. However, we do all need to be very careful when criticising others. The Bible clearly says that, when we point the finger at someone's sin, we are pointing that same finger at ourselves. This is because we can identify with those sins; we are familiar with them. People who have given up smoking are usually far less tolerant of smokers than are those who have never taken up the habit. Satan, in his customary way of bending the truth, insists that if we criticise homosexuals, then we must be latent homosexuals ourselves. In contrast, the Holy Spirit may gently remind us of a time when we were vulnerable to lapses of a heterosexual

SECTION 12

nature. We must therefore be very gentle when we encounter sin in others, especially when we are reminded that our own history has not been perfect.

The world is now under the rule of many people who no longer attend church. In the past, those making important decisions regularly encountered God's Word. The Bible used to form the basis of our laws. These days, human rights and political correctness seem to take precedence over everything. We now live in a humanist, secular world. However, please let us not contaminate God's churches with worldly opinions, or we will all be back again under the influence of the tree of knowledge of good and evil, where the wisdom of God is substituted by the fallen standards of the world – a world that is enjoying the rule of Satan.

And it is not just those in positions of authority; most people are now living their lives without the background of God's Word to guide their actions and their feelings. Yes, I know that many churches that are spiritually 'alive' have shown a huge increase in their congregations. I am still making comparison with the days when the average person felt it was his 'duty' to attend church. The last forty years or so have shown us just what the human heart is capable of in those who do not have regular access to God's Word.

Following the 11th September 2001 terrorist attacks, Anne Graham Lotz, Billy Graham's daughter, was interviewed on the CBS "The Early Show" when she was asked; "How could God let something like this happen?" Her answer has been quite widely circulated, but as I feel everybody should read it, I repeat it here in its entirety:

The Liberal Church

"I believe that God is deeply saddened by this, just as we are, but for years we've been telling God to get out of our schools, to get out of our government, and to get out of our lives. And, being the Gentleman that He is, I believe that He has calmly backed out. How can we expect God to give us His blessing and His protection if we demand that He leave us alone?

Let's see, I think it started when Madalyn Murray O'Hair – she was murdered, her body was found recently – complained she didn't want any prayer in our schools, and we said, OK.

Then, someone said you better not read the Bible in school ... the Bible that says thou shalt not kill; thou shalt not steal, and love your neighbour as yourself. And we said, OK.

Then, Dr. Benjamin Spock said we shouldn't spank our children when they misbehave because their little personalities would be warped and we might damage their self-esteem (Dr. Spock's son committed suicide.) And we said, an expert should know what he's talking about, so we said OK.

Then, someone said teachers and principals better not discipline our children when they misbehave. And the school administrators said no faculty member in this school better touch a student when they misbehave because we don't want any bad publicity, and we surely don't want to be sued. (There's a big difference between disciplining and touching, beating, smacking, humiliating, kicking, etc.) And we said, OK.

Then someone said, let's let our daughters have abortions if they want, and they won't even have to tell their parents. And we said, OK.

SECTION 12

> Then some wise school-board member said, Since boys will be boys and they're going to do it anyway, let's give our sons all the condoms they want, so they can have all the fun they desire, and we won't have to tell their parents they got them at school. And we said, OK.
> Then some of our top elected officials said it doesn't matter what we do in private as long as we do our jobs. And, agreeing with them, we said it doesn't matter to me what anyone, including the President, does in private as long as I have a job and the economy is good.
> And then, the entertainment industry said, let's make TV shows and movies that promote profanity, violence, and illicit sex. And, let's record music that encourages rape, drugs, murder, suicide and satanic themes. And we said, it's just entertainment, it has no adverse effect, and nobody takes it seriously anyway, so go right ahead.
> Now, we're asking ourselves why our children have no conscience, why they don't know right from wrong, and why it doesn't bother them to kill strangers, their classmates, and themselves. Probably, if we think about it long and hard enough, we can figure it out. I think it has a great deal to do with: 'We reap what we sow'."

A copy of those words should be placed on the desk of every politician, every sociologist and every teacher. They should also be compulsory reading for every parent – and every liberal clergyman!

I do agree that fundamentalism and fanaticism should be considered ugly words these days. Advocates of such extremes are usually concentrating on themselves – on how righteously they believe, instead of forgetting self and focusing on Jesus. Please believe me: I am not advocating a return to Puritan values. Entertainment and recreation are good for us.

The Liberal Church

Wholesome laughter and comedy really are a tonic and a gift from God. "Rejoice always" is virtually an order from God! Yes, artists should still capture the beauty of the human form, and writers such as D H Lawrence should still offer us their books. God will tell each of our hearts what is not acceptable to Him. He does not want to hide from us the basest facts of life. Let's face it: if the whole of the Bible were committed to a cinema screen, it would require at least an 'X' certificate! God has always given people a free will. He never banned anything – not in the sense that he removed all harmful influences from the world. Instead, He guides us so that we willingly keep some things out of our lives.

Of course, there are still many rough edges to my life – but I do now try to be open before God. It does indeed take a lifetime to complete someone's sanctification, and our Father knows just how long we all have! We must try to believe God's Word, and if He does call something we are doing detestable, then we must indeed ask Jesus for His help. Remember, every victory won in His strength is a blow against Satan.

Some claim that the matter of the ordination of women is less straightforward; they feel this to be an area where the Bible is unclear. The main cause of problems seems to be the passage at I Timothy 2: 12, where Paul tells us that he does not allow a woman to teach. In fact, if from verse 8 of this chapter, the words 'man' and 'woman' were translated 'husband' and 'wife', as they legitimately could be, then I believe the problems on this subject disappear. God is here talking about the relationship between a man with his wife during church fellowship, not about women preachers. God has clearly bestowed His gifts on many wonderful women. Women have been used by God to bring countless individuals to salvation in Jesus. Who would want to undo that? ... Not I.

SECTION 12

One thing that Jesus had to address, and something that is still a problem today, is the fact that some groups are more concerned about their traditions than they are about their relationship with the Lord. *" 'They worship Me in vain; their teachings are but rules taught by men.' You have let go of the commands of God and are holding on to the traditions of men"* (Mark 7: 7-8). Sadly, there are still many today who are more into 'Churchianity' than Christianity! I would strongly advise any thinking of joining a particular congregation to enquire first whether that Church is grounded in the Bible. New Christians are in need of a thriving fellowship in Jesus Christ, not a conservation society, social club or political wing! Thomas Cranmer, one of the pillars of the early Anglican Church, admitted that the Word of God is above the Church. C H Spurgeon adds: "The Bible, the whole Bible, and nothing but the Bible is the religion of Christ's Church."

Well, I did warn you! This has indeed been a very opinionated section. I should perhaps add that those whom I have acknowledged in the introductions to these books do not necessarily share all of the opinions given above, or indeed anywhere else in this series. Nor do the publishers of this work necessarily share all of the above opinions.

Many of God's children feel angry with some of the things that are said and done in the name of Jesus. The Bible needs no revision. It does not need to be updated or, heaven forbid, politically corrected!

God has revealed as much of Himself as He wants to in His Word. In it, Jesus Christ is shown to be God incarnate. Jesus came to show us God by His words, His miracles, His compassion ... His life! Jesus died, and we can now read His will; we can see just what He has left each one of us who now belong to His family! He is risen, and, through His Holy Spirit, now lives in the hearts of those who truly believe. These hearts

The Liberal Church

know the Bible to be the priceless, living Word of God; and so, I pray, do you.

Timothy Dwight tells us that the Bible "is a window in this prison world through which we may look into eternity." Yes, God's Word lifts you above this hectic satanic world. It gives you peace and unbroken fellowship with eternity. And when eternity is finally yours, you shall look back over the footprints you have made on this journey and rue those times when you actually believed that you were left on your own!

"When you walk through the waters
I'll be with you;
you will never sink beneath the waves.
When the fire is burning all around you,
you will never be consumed by the flames.

When the fear of loneliness is looming,
then remember, I am at your side.
When you dwell in the exile of the stranger,
remember you are precious in My eyes.

Do not be afraid,
for I have redeemed you.
I have called you by your name;
you are Mine.

You are Mine, O My child; I am your Father,
and I love you with a perfect love."

(Gerald Markland)

"For He chose us in Him
before the creation of the world
to be holy and blameless in His sight."
(Eph 1: 4)

"The Lord knows those who are His"
(2 Tim 2: 19)

Epilogue

The Lord has carefully preserved the oldest part of His Word for nearly three thousand years; the newest He has kept safe for two thousand years, in spite of attempts by Roman emperors to destroy every copy in existence. He has now placed it in your hands. Before He created a single piece of dust God knew that one day you would read what He has to say to you. He has waited for this moment, and now He eagerly awaits your response, for God's love is not complete until it has been reciprocated.

Now that you have taken God's Word into your heart through the indwelling Holy Spirit, you can now abide in that Word, for that Word is Jesus. He is God's written Word; He is God's risen Word. That same Word will now inform and inhabit your prayers, and you will know that your prayers are in accordance with God's will. Your faith in your prayer life will grow, and your Heavenly Father will be able to use you. You will then fulfil God's design for you. Through your faithful prayers, you will help move mountains of sin and doubt for the kingdom of God – and all heaven is delighted at the prospect!

Yes, the Word became flesh and made His dwelling among us. The Word died for you. The Word has risen and His Spirit lives in you. That Spirit will never die.
God keeps His Word!

"The Lord bless you and keep you;
The Lord make His face shine upon you
and be gracious to you;
The Lord turn His face towards you;
and give you peace."
(Num 6: 24-26)

Also Available
(In the same format)

Part One: **Saved by God**
  Coming close to the Cross

Forthcoming
Part Three: **Heard by God**
  Being stilled by God in Prayer

www.ingramcontent.com/pod-product-compliance
Lightning Source LLC
Chambersburg PA
CBHW071518040426
42444CB00008B/1702